Chinese Communists
and Rural Society,
1927-1934

A publication of the
Center for Chinese Studies
University of California,
Berkeley, California 94720

Cover Colophon by Shih-hsiang Chen

Center for Chinese Studies • CHINA RESEARCH MONOGRAPHS
UNIVERSITY OF CALIFORNIA, BERKELEY

*NUMBER THIRTEEN*

# CHINESE COMMUNISTS AND RURAL SOCIETY, 1927-1934

PHILIP C. C. HUANG
LYNDA SCHAEFER BELL
KATHY LEMONS WALKER

50113

Although the Center for Chinese Studies is responsible for the selection and acceptance of monographs in this series, responsibility for the opinions expressed in them and for the accuracy of statements contained in them rests with their authors.

© 1978 by the Regents of the University of California
ISBN 0-912966-18-1
Library of Congress Catalog Number 78-620018
Printed in the United States of America
$5.00

# Contents

INTRODUCTION .............................. 1
    Philip C. C. Huang

INTELLECTUALS, LUMPENPROLETARIANS,
WORKERS AND PEASANTS IN THE
COMMUNIST MOVEMENT ..................... 5
    Philip C. C. Huang

AGRICULTURAL LABORERS AND
    RURAL REVOLUTION ........................ 29
    Lynda Schaefer Bell

THE PARTY AND PEASANT WOMEN ........... 57
    Kathy LeMons Walker

A COMMENT ON THE WESTERN LITERATURE . 83
    Philip C. C. Huang

REFERENCES ................................ 99

GLOSSARY .................................. 117

LIST OF MAPS
  I. Revolutionary Base Areas and Guerilla Zones in 1934  2
  II. The Central Soviet Area in 1934 .............. 6
  III. Xingguo and Surrounding Counties ............ 10

# The Jiangxi Period[1]: an Introduction
Philip C. C. Huang

The Chinese Communist movement in its early years was primarily urban-based. Radical intellectuals in the cities made up the original core of the movement, concentrating their efforts on organizing industrial workers in major cities like Shanghai, Nanchang, Wuhan and Canton [Guangzhou]. The result was that urban intellectuals and workers constituted the overwhelming majority of the 58,000 party members in April 1927—22% and 60%, respectively (Harrison, 1972: 70; Han. 1972: 212). The peasant association movement of the mid-1920's, in spite of the large membership claimed (as of June, 1927 4.5 million members in Hunan, 2.5 million in Hubei, and 700,000 in Guangdong — Diyici, 1953: 18-19), remained marginal to the movement as a whole, as shown by the fact that peasants accounted for only 5% of party members in April 1927 (Harrison, 1972: 70).

In the years after 1927, however, the social base of the party was to change drastically. Party ranks were decimated by counter-revolutionary suppression (down to 10,000 at the end of 1927), with most of the surviving members driven into the countryside. There, severed from the proletarian base built earlier, the movement had almost to start anew.

Most intellectuals in the movement had had little or no contact with peasants. Even the few, like Mao Ze-dong, who had experience in the earlier peasant association movement, found that they had to operate under entirely different conditions: the earlier movement had been based primarily in the vicinity of major urban centers, which the communists now had to avoid because counter-revolutionary power was strongest there. The earlier movement had also ridden the tide of military victory, absorbing vast numbers of peasant association members along the route of the Northern Expedition (Huang, 1975: 281); now communists were hunted everywhere — the larger bands by Chiang Kai-shek's [Jiang Jie-shi] or his affiliated warlords' armies; the smaller cells by the local police or landlords' militia.

Under such conditions, the path of least resistance for the communists would have been simply to degenerate into banditry, as so many rebels had done before in Chinese history. An armed band could hole up in a mountain

---

[1] I use the term here to refer to the entire period from October 1927 to October 1934, when the main movement under Mao was operating in Jiangxi province.

## I. REVOLUTIONARY BASE AREAS AND GUERILLA ZONES IN 1934[a]

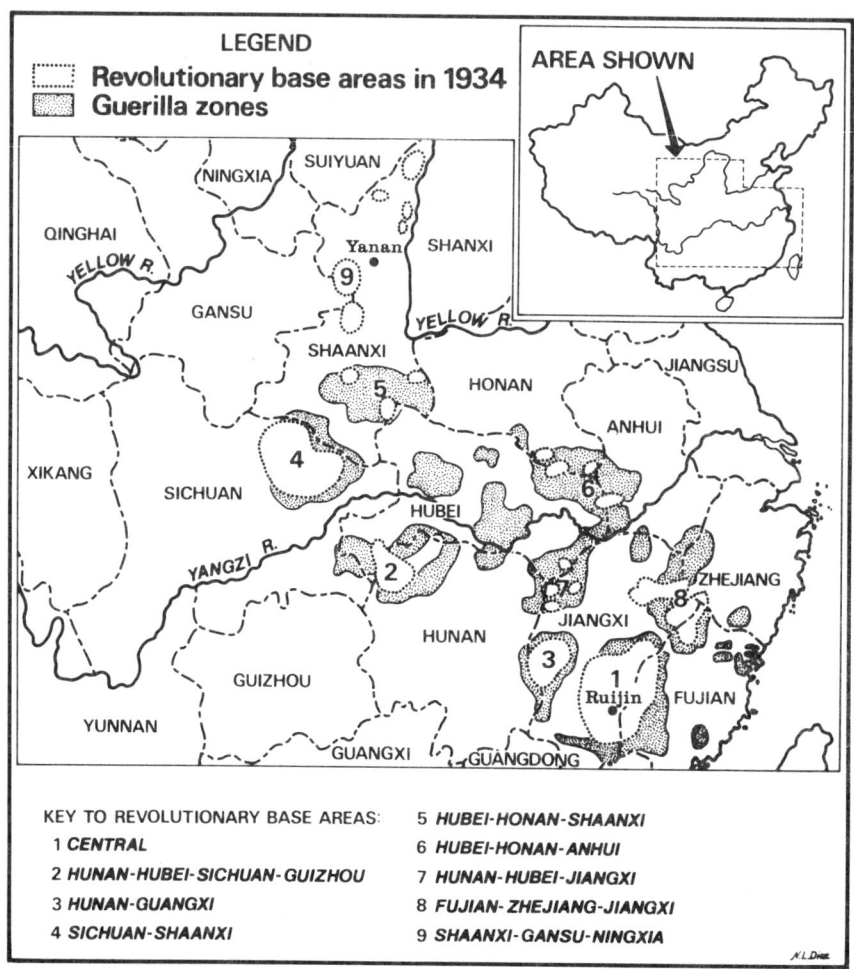

KEY TO REVOLUTIONARY BASE AREAS:
1 *CENTRAL*
2 *HUNAN-HUBEI-SICHUAN-GUIZHOU*
3 *HUNAN-GUANGXI*
4 *SICHUAN-SHAANXI*
5 *HUBEI-HONAN-SHAANXI*
6 *HUBEI-HONAN-ANHUI*
7 *HUNAN-HUBEI-JIANGXI*
8 *FUJIAN-ZHEJIANG-JIANGXI*
9 *SHAANXI-GANSU-NINGXIA*

[a]Based on *Peking Review*, 45 (Nov. 7), 1975: 11

stronghold, as indeed Mao did in the Jinggang Mountains on the Hunan-Jiangxi border in 1928, and conduct forays into nearby villages and towns for supplies. Or it could stay on the move, as Zhu De and Peng Dehuai did until they joined up with Mao in the Jinggang Mountains, and draw their recruits mainly from the dispossessed, unemployed and criminal elements—the lumpenproletariat—that crowded the market towns and "floated" on the villages (such people number 20 million at this time, in Mao's estimate) (Mao, 1926: 171-172). Bandits and warlords had typically built up their armies this way.

Those communists who perceived these potential trends toward banditry and warlordism advocated two different solutions. Qu Qiu-bai, who led the party Central in Shanghai from August 1927 to April 1928, called for a return to the cities at all costs. Li Li-san, who succeeded Qu and formulated party policy from June to September 1930 thought the same: in his view, for the communist movement to become a rural-based movement was tantamount to losing its revolutionary character; it must return to its proper social base — the urban proletariat (Mao, 1945 "Guanyu . . .": 961-962; Rue, 1966: 138). From Qu and Li came the orders for the hasty attempts to seize major cities in 1927, and again in 1930. Facing overwhelmingly superior military force, those uprisings had no chance of success. Their defeat only added further to the pressures toward banditry and warlordism. The alternative approach, advocated by Mao, was to correct such tendencies by building stable base areas, by rooting down into the natural villages and drawing on the revolutionary energies of poor peasants.

The second strategy turned out to be successful. In spite of tremendous military pressures from Chiang Kai-shek's five successive "encircle and exterminate" campaigns (that mobilized a whopping one million men by the Fifth Campaign—Snow, 1938: 186), the party was able to grow from its low of 10,000 members at the end of 1927 to 300,000 members by the beginning of 1934. By that time, nine "soviets" (a word that came to mean not just worker-peasant congresses but also "revolutionary bases") had been built, with a total population of over nine million (see Map I). The largest base was the Central Soviet Area (with its capital at Ruijin, Jiangxi—hence the term "the Jiangxi period" or "the Jiangxi Soviet") built under Mao and Zhu De's leadership. At the beginning of 1934, it encompassed most of sixteen counties *(xian)* and a population of 3 million (Snow, 1938: 73).

It was in these base areas, rather than Shanghai where the Party Central was headquartered (until it moved to the Central Soviet Area in January 1933), that the communist movement faced up to the challenge of adapting to new conditions, learning to work with rural social groups, who comprised the majority of the Chinese population, thus making the transition from an urban-based movement to a rural-based one.

It was not an easy process, as I have already suggested, and as the three articles[2] that follow will show. In Xingguo county, as I attempt to illustrate in my article, the intellectuals at first found their most ready allies in the gamblers and salt smugglers who hung around the market towns. Although these lumpenproletarians acted as the cutting edge of the revolutionary attack on the established order, transformation of this group as a whole into disciplined party cadres proved impossible. Years of systematic effort were required, first through land reform and then through the construction of new political organs in the villages, to activate the farming population and thus change the social composition of the movement from lumpenproletarian to poor peasant. In the course of these efforts, as Lynda Bell's article shows, some party intellectuals were burdened with excessively literal interpretations of the concept of proletarian leadership. These individuals, who dominated the Party Central from January 1931 to January 1935, sought to superimpose that notion on the countryside by identifying agricultural workers and coolies as the proletariat in the rural areas. The problem with attempting to build the movement in this way was that such a "rural proletariat" numbered at best 10% of the rural population and were often viewed as outcasts by poor peasants. Consequently, they were adequate neither in numbers nor in their relationship with the rest of rural society to form the core of the movement. Another major obstacle was the domesticated inertia of the female half of the population, an inertia born of a system in which women were mere property to be kept inside the house. Kathy Walker's article details the party's efforts to activate peasant women behind the tasks of revolution and civil war.

This volume is about these years of trial and error in the movement's transition from a primarily proletarian social base to a poor peasant one. The focus is on the interaction between communist intellectuals and rural social classes and groups. From that interaction was to emerge the shape of the larger social movement that became the Chinese Revolution.

Specialists of the history of the Revolution might prefer to read the final article first. I review there past studies of the Jiangxi period and discuss the rationale behind the approach taken here: most past research has concentrated on top-level power struggles and line disputes; our emphasis here is on the social basis and social content of the movement.

[2] Bell's, Walker's and my articles began as papers in a writing seminar which I conducted at UCLA in 1974-75. Originally intended to last only two quarters, the seminar grew into almost a "Jiangxi project" that has continued for two years. The three of us have all benefited from each other's research and ideas.

# Intellectuals, Lumpenproletarians, Workers and Peasants in the Communist Movement:

the Case of Xingguo County, 1927-1934*

Philip C.C. Huang

The center of gravity of the Chinese revolutionary movement shifted from the cities to the countryside in 1927. How did the Communist Party, with its urban origins and largely urban membership, interact with different rural classes and groups after 1927? This article presents some tentative answers to this question by looking at a single county, a level at which we can analyze not only party "lines" and policies, but their social basis and how they translated into action.

## Intellectuals and Lumpenproletarians

In remote southern Jiangxi, where the Central Soviet Area (see Map II) was to be situated, the Communist Party had only made a very modest beginning before the counterrevolution struck in 1927. Urban organizing work had only begun in August 1926, largely within the city of Ganzhou (which had a population of about 200,000—Cressey, 1955: 186). In March, the party-sponsored Ganzhou Labor Union claimed a membership of 16,000 workers. Rural organizing did not begin until November 1926, after the province had been secured under the Northern Expedition Army. In May 1927, the Jiangxi Provincial Peasant Association claimed a membership of 380,000, compared with a reported total of more than four million in Hunan (Diyici, 1953: 18, 413, 421). There were possibly several hundred party members operating in southern Jiangxi.[1]

*Author's note: my thanks to Jerome Chen, Linda Grove, Ilpyong Kim and John Rue who commented on a rough draft of this article in the summer of 1975.

## II. THE CENTRAL SOVIET AREA IN 1934

Counterrevolutionary suppression began on March 12, the second anniversary of Sun Yat-sen's death. On that day, Chen Xiang-zhih (also known as Chen Zan-xian), chief party organizer in southern Jiangxi and head of the Ganzhou Labor Union, was invited to join in a memorial service for Sun. On arrival, Chen was gunned down. In April, the Ganzhou Labor Union headquarters was burnt down, and party members scattered underground (Yi-lan, 1958; Chen Qi-han, 1958: 407-408). In southern Jiangxi, as elsewhere, the party had almost to start afresh, this time in the rural hinterland rather than the major urban centers and their vicinities.

Local party branches and cells had to survive on their own as best they could. Few could even maintain contact with higher level party units. None in southern Jiangxi had the option of joining a stable base area; none had the military forces with which to build a base area. Hounded by White armies and police, individual members and cells sought cover and allies wherever they could. Many were to turn to the local secret society, the Three Dots (San-dian Hui).

The Three Dots in Xingguo were an offshoot of the Triads in Guangdong, probably with connections through the salt traffic. Southern Jiangxi relied entirely on Guangdong for its salt. From Xingguo, porters carried chickens to sell in Meixian in northeastern Guangdong, bought salt with the proceeds, and returned to Xingguo to sell the salt, a journey that took 20 to 30 days. To take conditions in 1930 as an example: a one-person load of salt could bring the porter a net profit of about 13 *yuan* (3 yuan could buy 100 catties of rice). The *lijin* [likin] tax burden on such a load was 2.80 yuan, or more than 20%. (Mao, 1931.1.26: 211.) There was thus great temptation to avoid the lijin check points (of which there were six between Xingguo and Meixian)—in other words, to smuggle. Under such conditions, the elaborate salt smuggling network of the Triads in Guangdong (Hsieh, 1972) readily extended into the market towns of southern Xingguo as well.

Like most Triad lodges, the Three Dots of Xingguo thus had one foot deeply into the criminal underworld. Fragmentary evidence (see discussion of Yong-feng district [qu] below) suggests that they were also involved in opium and gambling. The lodge's membership, accordingly, consisted of substantial numbers of bandits, smugglers, gamblers, and vagabonds—lumpenproletarians.

At the same time, the Three Dots of Xingguo shared with the Triads of Guangdong a strongly political heritage. Time and time again the Triads had led popular uprisings against the Manchu dynasty and against the established order. They had played a prominent role in popular uprisings before and during the Revolution of 1911 (Hsieh, 1972; Lust, 1972). In such activities, leadership seems to have come more often from intellectuals and the proto-proletariat—coolies, itinerant artisans, boatmen, and so on (Chesneaux, 1971).

This dual political and criminal characteristic of the societies made them almost as likely to be against the revolution as for it. On the one hand, their rebel heritage and outlaw membership made them ready allies of the political fugitive. They were also often the only popular organization that stretched beyond the immediate market town and had a membership whose experience went beyond the confines of peasant life. On the other hand, as criminal gangs, they could be controlled and used by anyone who could afford the price. The Green Gang *(Qing Bang)* of Shanghai is one ready example: they became willing henchmen and butchers for Chiang Kai-shek's [Jiang Jie-shi] massacre of communists and progressives in Shanghai. In the Three Dots organization in Xingguo, the ten Duan brothers, led by one Duan Qi-feng, had been similarly used: former bandits, they had hired themselves out to lead the attack on the Communists' headquarters in Ganzhou in April 1927 (Chen Qi-han, 1958).

The Communist Party branch in Xingguo, however, was not in a position to be too choosy. Several of the party members had good connections with the lodge, which they decided to exploit for shelter for party members on the run. Before long, the local party committee decided to exploit the connections further. By the spring of 1928, party members had managed to gain control over most of the powerful positions in the society. They then succeeded in establishing the party's authority within the lodge by executing several unruly lodge members to set an example. After that, the Xingguo party organization simply absorbed the lodge's membership en masse, including the ten Duan brothers. Any available ally was welcome in the desperate situation of 1927-28.

The account written by Chen Qi-han, leader of the party organization in the county at this time (and a member of the Tenth Central Committee of the Party today), further shows that this local party of fugitive revolutionary intellectuals combined with local lumpenproletarians in fact behaved not too differently from social bandits. In April 1928, the Xingguo organization managed to seize and hold the county seat for several days. But the communists did little more than issue a few slogans, march some big gentry around town, and forcibly extract loans from the town merchants. There was no attempt at systematic establishment of a revolutionary government.

When Mao Ze-dong and Zhu De arrived (from Jinggangshan) with their Red Fourth Army in March 1929, they tried to rectify the situation. They left a few seasoned cadres to work with the Xingguo organization, and instructed Chen Qi-han and his followers to attempt to build representative bodies (soviets) on the district and township levels (Xingguo county [xian] at this time consisted of twelve districts [qu] each divided into several townships [xiang] which in turn comprised several villages [cun] each). Mao, apparently, tried to impress the importance of rallying mass support upon the rather unsophisticated local leadership by telling them: "You must chant every day 'rally mass support, rally mass support, rally. . .' the way a monk repeats 'amida buddha, amida. . .'." This was revolutionary theory adapted for lumpenproletarians.

But Xingguo fell again to the White forces almost as soon as Mao and Zhu left to continue their march to Ruijin, and the local party had once more to concern itself with survival and mobility above all else. For the next ten months, they carried on sporadic guerilla warfare in the county. There could be no opportunity for building stable organizations and the revolutionary movement remained largely a movement of urban intellectuals and rural outcasts, drifting on the surface of the countryside (Chen Qi-han, 1958: 407-417).

With the arrival of Chen Yi's Third Column of the Red Army in late 1929, Xingguo was finally secured under revolutionary power for a period of 16 months. Only then was the party able to anchor down and, as I shall show in the next sections, to reach beneath the market towns into the farming population in the villages through land reform and the establishment of new village-run political organs.

But even after land reform the upper and middle levels of the county government and party organization were for a time still dominated by urban intellectuals and lumpenproletarians. The district of Yongfeng (see Map III), on which complete information is available, may or may not be an extreme example: of eighteen individuals who staffed the district government after land reform in 1930, eight had been professional gamblers, and one a Daoist priest; the other nine included three intellectuals, one doctor, one "laboring woman," one tailor, two rich peasants, and one "unknown." The seven people identified by Mao in his detailed report as the most powerful were:

> Chairman: Xiao Zhi-chun. "Did not farm; sold chickens, traveling to Guangdong; gambler; watchman at the ancestral temple; no house of his own; cannot read much; joined the revolution year before last."
> Judge: Liu Shao-biao. "(Had served as Chairman until July.) Did not farm;

## III. XINGGUO AND SURROUNDING COUNTIES

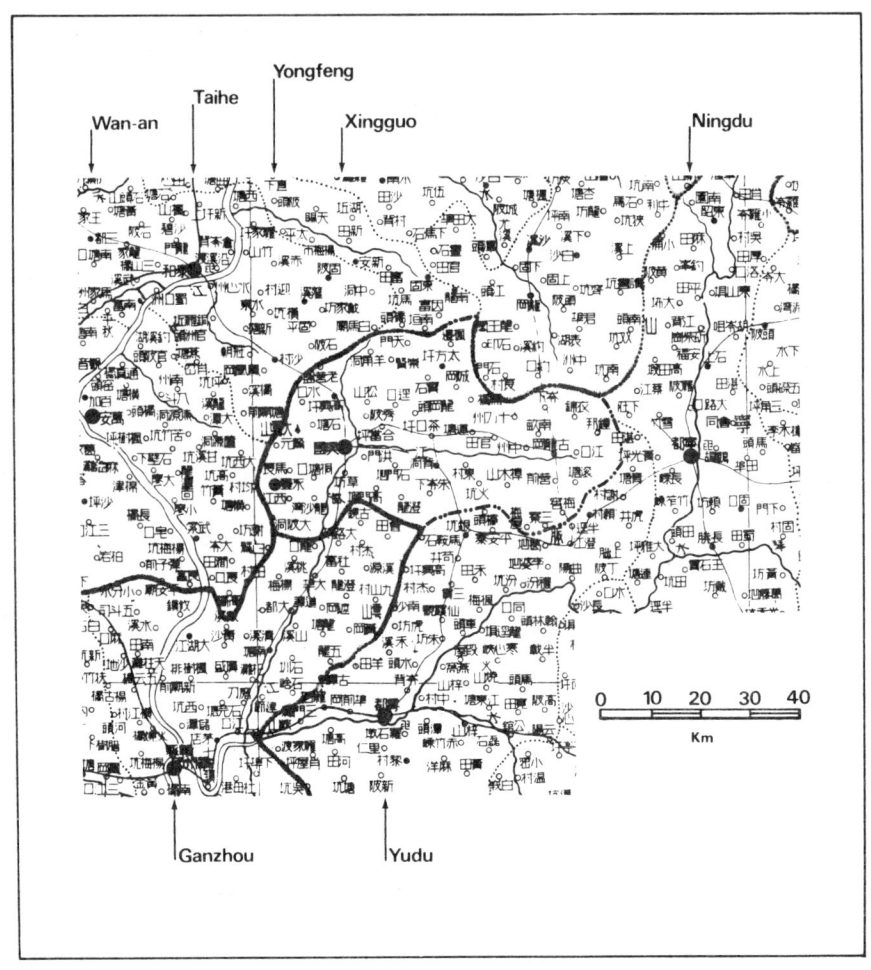

Xingguo county population in 1932: 231,286 *(Hongse Zhonghua,* 41 (1932.11.21): 5.

studied fighting; can read a little; worked as a tailor for a time. . ., then became a professional gambler, joined the revolution year before last."
Treasurer: Liu Shao-ming. "Doctor. . .joined the revolution year before last."
Propaganda Officer: Wang Zhen-ren.". . .had no work; made a living by gambling; joined the revolution year before last. . ."
Secretary: Xie Ying-shan. "Educated. . ."
? Chen Gun-tong. ". . .middle peasant and gambler, illiterate; joined the revolution year before last. . ."
Cultural Officer: Zou Li-dong. ". . .bankrupt landlord; college graduate; joined the revolution year before last. . ."
Judge: Leng Li-bang. ". . .Daoist priest. . .joined the revolution year before last, and later commanded guerilla units. . ." (Mao, 1931.1.26: 241-244.)

Four professional gamblers, two intellectuals, and one Daoist priest. All had joined the revolution "year before last," 1928, the year the party absorbed the entire Three Dots membership. In short, the Xingguo party in the years of confusion between 1927 and 1930 was very much a party of intellectuals and lumpenproletarians, the product of a simple merger between the county party organization and the local Three Dots.

The question must be asked: Was this prominence of lumpenproletarians unique to the Xingguo party organization?

I think not, and would speculate that this was a persistent tendency in the movement, a tendency that became very widespread in the years 1927 to 1930. Even in the earlier Hunan peasant movement, as Mao's own report made clear, lumpenproletarians predominated: in Hengshan county, lumpenproletarians (which Mao called the "red poor" *(chipin)*, who were "completely unemployed, who had neither land nor capital. . . and had to become soldiers, or go off and sell their labor, or drift about as beggars, or. . .become bandits or thieves," and who totalled twenty of every seventy of the "poor") occupied half of the posts in the township peasant associations. Mao went on to make clear that he thought the Hengshan example was representative of the movement as a whole (Mao, 1927.3.28: 218-219).

As for the period we are discussing, it is well known that when Mao reached the Jinggang mountains in October 1927, after the Autumn Harvest uprisings, he made an alliance with the local bandit group, led by Wang Zuo and Yan Wen-cai, two Triad members (Snow, 1938: 170; Schram, 1966). It is also well-known that Zhu De was a ranking member of the Ge-lao Hui, the most powerful society in the Yangzi [Yangtze] valley (Smedley, 1956: 88-89). He no doubt took advantage of his Ge-lao Hui connections in building the armed forces that he led up to Jinggang. As Mao pointed out in his report to the Party Central in November 1928: the Red Army had had to draw many of its recruits from among the *youmin* (literally, the floating people). As a result, "roving banditism" *(liukou zhuhi)* had become one of the main problems in the Red Army (Mao, 1928.12: 37). At the Gutian Conference a year later, Mao referred still more clearly to this problem and pointed out that "the lumpenproletariat *(youmin wuchanjieji)* constitute the majority *(zhan daduoshu)* in the Red Army."[2] He went on to suggest that every effort should be made to recruit workers and peasants into the army in order to rectify the class composition of the army. (Mao, 1929.12: 90, 91.)

Other examples can be cited. He Long returned to western Hunan after the defeat at Swatow to build an army that eventually became the Second Front Red Army, with 40,000 guns by 1935. His stature in the Ge-lao Hui of the Hunan countryside was crucial to his effectiveness in that task (Snow, 1938: 58-62). Liu Zhi-dan, who built the Shaan-Gan-Ning base area, was a figure much like He Long—also a member of the Ge-lao Hui (Snow, 1938: 219-225). In 1936, Mao was to issue a formal appeal in the name of the Central Committee to this most powerful of China's secret societies for a united front against Japan (Schram, 1966).

By then the party had learned that the secret society connection had a double edge. The dual political and criminal character of the societies meant that there was always plenty of room for rascals and opportunists, such as the ten Duan brothers who were absorbed into the Xingguo party organization in 1928.

In fact, by 1930 the Duan brothers and other lumpenproletarians had entrenched themselves not only in the party organization in Xingguo (as shown in the case of Yongfeng district), but in the provincial levels of the party and the government as well. Although the full details may never be known, the struggle against opportunistic lumpenproletarians such as the Duan brothers was clearly an important, if little mentioned, part of the intense factional strife in the party during these years.

That there was intense intra-party strife should not be surprising. After all, the party had been badly splintered in 1927, with scattered groups, branches and cells each going their own way and finding support wherever they could. Under such conditions, factional strife was unavoidable. And factional divisions rendered the party as a whole extremely vulnerable to disruptions and subversion by Guomindang agents, which in turn further aggravated factionalism.

These struggles exploded into the open toward the end of 1930 and became linked to the principal policy dispute of the time: between the policy of seizing major urban centers, advocated by the Party Central in Shanghai headed by Li Li-san, and the policy of building rural base areas, identified with Mao and Zhu De (Mao, 1945 "Guanyu. . .": 961-

963). Mao made the first move in November. He arrested some 4,400 officers and men in the Red Army and almost all members of the party's Western and Southern Jiangxi Action Committee. On December 7 or 8, one Liu Di, battlion political commissar of the 20th army, revolted with 400 men, seized the town of Futian, and released the arrested men from prison. In this revolt, which came to be known as the "Futian Incident," some 1,800 of Mao's followers were killed and many arrested, including Kang Ke-qing, Zhu De's wife. The rebels overthrew the Jiangxi provincial soviet govenment headquartered in Futian, set up a rival soviet government, and called for Mao's overthrow. But Zhu De, Peng Dehuai, and Huang Gong-lue, who commanded most of the military forces of the base area, came out solidly in support of Mao. Defeated, the Futian rebels escaped across the Gan River, while Li Li-san's leadership of the Party Central was terminated (Hsiao, 1961: 98-113; Rue, 1966: 231-237; Han, 1972: 234-235).

Duan Qi-feng, the real leader behind the Futian Incident, was not identified as such until after his arrest and trial in 1933. Only then did the party learn that Duan had been the top agent in Jiangxi of the Guomindang's secret "Anti-Bolshevik" (AB) League *(Hongse Zhonghua,* 1933.6.14; Cao Bo-yi, 1969: 427). Among those under his command was one Xiao Zi-zheng, Secretary of the Xingguo party committee! *(Hongse Zhonghua,* 1932.4.21: 8; Lötveit, 1973: 100)

Xingguo is possibly a rather extreme example. But the case illustrates well the tremendous pressures upon the different party units at this time. Faced with constant White military and police pressure, it was much easier for party members and cells to stay on the move than to try to root down in the villages. The fugitive radical intellectual on the run, in turn, found the already uprooted, the rural outcasts—the lumpenproletarians—the most readily available ally. At the same time, the Party Central at this time continued to stress cities above the contryside, a reflection of the biases of many urban intellectuals in the party. It was a policy that discouraged systematic efforts to penetrate and organize the farming population. Furthermore, the Party Central's unrealistic calls for armed uprisings to seize the major cities only further encouraged indiscriminate recruitment of party members. The tendency toward degenerating into a roving bandit group of fugitive urban intellectuals and rural lumpenproletarians was thus very strong. It was a tendency that required years of systematic effort to overcome.

### The Land Revolution

Land reform in southern Jiangxi began after the February 7 (1930) conference of top communist leaders in the area convened by Mao. Although the conference did not promulgate a land law, it did reach decisions for immediate redistribution of land. The target was complete equalization, by using two principles: "take from those with excess to compensate those who do not have enough" *(chouduo bushao)*, and "take from fertile land to compensate lean land" (so that no one would hold only fertile land while others had only lean land) *(choufei bushou)*. In this process, not only landlords' land but also rich peasants' land was to be redistributed. These principles for land distribution were identified with Mao (Mao, 1945 "Guanyu...": 974; Hsiao, 1969: 17-22; Rue, 1966: 189-203, 300-304).

What actually happened in land reform varied considerably from place to place. As we have seen, the party apparatus at this time had not yet penetrated the villages but remained largely at the level of the market town and above; it still lacked the organization and the experience to implement land reform in any systematic or uniform way. Much depended on the local leadership and local conditions. In many places, as Mao observed, rich and middle peasants were able to co-opt the revolutionary movement and retained their privileged positions. In such villages, no real change in the power structure occurred (Mao, 1930.11.15: 166-167). At the same time, many rich peasants gave up only their worst land under the principle of *chouduo bushao* and were able to avoid the process of *choufei bushou*. Thus they continued to hold the best land in the village (Mao, 1931.1.26: 235; Mao, 1930.11.15: 167). In such situations, the old social and political relations in the villages remained largely intact, and the party stayed on the surface of the countryside.

It was in this context that the Provisional Land Law adopted by the Party Central in Shanghai in May 1930, under Li Li-san's leadership, became an issue of dispute. The Provisional Land Law was much easier on rich peasants than the intent of the February 7 conference: only that part of the land that rich peasants leased out was to be confiscated for redistribution (Hsiao, 1969: 127-130); rich peasants could, in other words, retain the land which they hired agricultural workers to cultivate. Since most rich peasants cultivated their surplus land with the use of agricultural workers rather than renting out their surplus land, the provisions of the Li Li-san Land Law meant in effect that most rich peasants would remain untouched by the land revolution.

In Xingguo, the effect of Li Li-san's Land Law (no doubt unintentionally) would simply have been counterrevolutionary. Here many landlords and rich peasants had organized armed bands to protect their interests against the roving communists. In Yongfeng district, for example, most of the nine (households of) resident landlords and thirty-two (households of) rich peasants had joined together to organize a militia *(Jingweituan)*. Class lines were already sharply drawn (Mao, 1931.1.26: 213-217). In such a polarized context, to protect rich peasant interests was to side with the established structures of power.

In Xingguo the social revolution in fact came quickly and violently. In the district of Yongfeng, three of the nine landlords and nine of the thirty-two rich peasants were killed during the land revolution. Most of the others ran away. Of those who remained, a few willingly burnt their land deeds and joined the side of the revolution; the rest were imprisoned (Mao, 1931.1.26: 213-217).

Land redistribution proceeded in like fashion. In the recollection of Chen Qi-han, the orders of the February 7 conference amounted to simply: "Divide! Fast!" Party branches and committees on the district and township levels were instructed to complete land redistribution in three days! (Chen Qi-han, 1958: 416; Mao, 1931.1.26: 233.)

The process was simple and direct. Each village received a half-day's notice alerting it to the arrival of a propagandist from the district government. A mass meeting was called, at which this cadre from the district government announced and explained the benefits of land reform and the methods by which it was to be carried out. At this same meeting, a chairman, a secretary, and other village functionaries were "elected." The key post was the head of the new "land department," which had responsibility for tallying up the existing land ownership and for working out the amount of land each person was to receive—arrived at by simply dividing the total amount of land (in weight of yield) by the number of people in the village. The results were then announced at a mass meeting; those who had more than their share were told at that meeting to decide on which portion of their land they would give up. In Yongfeng district, two of the townships completed redistribution in late March in the space of seven days, the other two in eight days, in a whirlwind that allowed neither opposition nor much participation from below (Mao, 1931.1.26: 233-235).

In May, further equalization was achieved by dividing the hillside land (the initial division in March had concentrated on cropland on flat grounds). In August, lineage estates and temple land was divided. And the principle of *choufei bushou* was now systematically applied to counter the problem of rich and middle peasants' retaining the most fertile land.

Different grades of land were carefully classified. Those who had a disproportionately large share of good land were asked to give up part of that land in exchange for poorer land. The target was complete equalization, with every household cultivating a mixture of different grades of land. By the time of Mao's report in October 1930, three of the four townships in Yongfeng had already completed this second division. Land reform there had been abrupt and thorough (Mao, 1931.1.26: 188-200, 236, 238).

The poor peasants, some 60% of the population in this area, of course benefited most immediately and dramatically from thorough land distribution.

Here in the South Yangzi Hills, land was relatively fertile—a second crop of rice could be raised on most of the irrigated land, by planting in alternate rows two weeks after the first planting. Had land been distributed evenly, each person would have averaged two *mu* (one mu = 1/6 acre) of cropland (Cressey, 1955: 188-190) and peasant families could certainly have derived minimal subsistence from the produce of their labor. But land was of course not evenly distributed. In Mao's figures for the period just prior to land reform, the poor peasants, 60% of the population, owned only 5% of the land. Almost all poor peasants, in other words, were landless tenants. This meant that they could only consume about one-half of what they produced, paying 50 to 60% of their produce to their landlord as rent. The result here, as in most parts of China, was that the poor could not afford to eat only the preferred fine grains (rice in south China; rice and polished wheat flour in the north), but had to rely on sweet potatoes to make up for the rice they could not afford (one dan of rice exchanged for three dan of sweet potatoes in Xingguo). The less fortunate simply went hungry.

The majority of the poor had to borrow money during the hungry months before harvest, and thus had to bear the burden also of high interest. Most borrowed from the rich peasants, at an interest of 20% per year. Those who could not come up with the security for a money loan turned to crop loans. The standard interest on such loans was an astronomical 50%, for a six to nine month loan between the hungry winter or spring months and the next harvest. Most crop borrowers turned to the "charitable" granaries *(yicang)*[3] of their lineages, which charged a somewhat less oppressive 30% (and accounted for 90% of all crop loans). For the most desperate borrowers, there were the pawn shops which gave a cash loan equal to one-half of the market value of the pawned item, redeemable within ten months at a rate of 5% interest per month. After ten months, one month's grace was allowed before forfeiture. Mao estimated that 60% of all poor peasants had had to turn to pawn shops (Mao, 1931.1.26: 203-212, 219-222).

The burden of debt, added to the burden of rent, meant a cycle of poverty and hunger from which there could be virtually no hope of escape, until, in one stroke, the land revolution equalized land ownership (thereby eliminating rent) and nullified all outstanding debts. For the poor peasants, the land revolution made the difference between hunger and a full stomach.

The other poor people in the villages—agricultural workers, beggars, prostitutes, vendors, and so on—also benefited from the land revolution. They had all been landless before the revolution; they now received a share of land equal to others. Vendors and other petty merchants who had run businesses on a shoestring (thirty-four of the forty-six shops in Yongfeng had been operated on a capital of betwen 10 yuan and 20 yuan) were allowed to participate in land division, some fully, some in part. After the revolution most continued to operate their businesses. And those businesses, since they were poor businesses run for poor people, did not suffer from the results of the levelling of income, as did the luxury services (Mao, 1931.1.26: 227-230).

It was among the village poor, therefore, that the party could expect the most willing support. Activists from the village poor were the ones who could be expected to serve as the link between the urban-originated party and the village population as a whole. They were the logical basis for the penetration of the party organization into the villages.

But the land revolution in itself also left substantial segments of the population indifferent or even hostile. In Yongfeng, the middle peasants constituted about 20% of the population and owned 15% of the land. For them, equalization brought only slight economic gains at best and was profoundly unsettling at worst; some, the most well-off middle peasants, had to give up land (Mao, 1931.1.26: 217). For this group, hostility or support for the revolution turned on political rather than economic reasons.

Artisans, 7% of the population in Yongfeng, were another substantial group for whom the economic effects of the revolution were ambiguous. Liquidation of the landlords and rich peasants brought a sharp decline in the demand for the service of tailors and bricklayers (two of the four most numerous categories of artisans), while demand for the work of tinsmiths and firecrackermakers, for lacquer work, portraits and religious images ceased altogether. Most of such disemployed artisans were allowed to receive land so that their livelihood was not threatened (Mao, 1931.1.26: 225-227). For those who had been part-time cultivators, the changeover from craftsman to farmer might not have been too painful. For the full-time and highly skilled artisans, however, the changeover must have created great tensions.

Together, middle peasants and artisans amounted to a sizeable and influential segment of the rural population. Unlike the landlords, who were a class entirely set apart from the villagers, the middle peasants' livelihood differed from the poor peasants' much less sharply. Nor did they engage in lending money at usurious rates like the rich peasants. They were not the objects of class antagonisms in the social revolution. Their attitudes during and after the revolution accordingly were far more influential on the poor. Often literate and better informed than the poor peasants, their influence easily could become disproportionate to their numbers.

In Xingguo, these problems were further complicated by the strength of lineage organizations. Lineages in southern Jiangxi were comparable in strength to those in southern Hunan, Guangdong, and eastern Guangxi (Sun, 1938: 1). In Yongfeng, lineage estates totalled 10% of all land and, as mentioned above, the lineage organizations operated "charitable" granaries and provided loan services. As might be expected, kinship ties were often a labyrinth that cut across class lines, and class revolution had therefore to contend with kinship allegiances. In the one case cited by Mao, Changjiao village of the "third" township in Yongfeng, lineage allegiances were so strong that in the first land division in March, villagers refused to redistribute land outside of the lineage; the first redivision was thus carried out only within each lineage group rather than in the village as a whole. Lineage lines were only breached in the distribution of hill land in August (Mao, 1931.1.26: 239).

Problems such as these could not be resolved by the arithmetic of material gain and loss. The question of the allegiance and support of middle peasants, and of the degree to which class revolution could successfully cut across lineage connections, were finally matters of morale and political leadership.

In this last respect the party in 1930 still suffered from serious weaknesses. As I already indicated in the first part of this article, the former lumpenproletarian members of the Three Dots remained prominent in the party organization, especially in its middle ranks— the provincial, county, and district levels. To a large extent, the post land-reform party organization in 1930 consisted of urban intellectuals at the central and higher levels of the party, lumpenproletarians at the middle levels (most of them recruited hurriedly in the two preceding years), and, finally, newly recruited peasant activists at the basic township and village levels.

The crucial weakness was in the lumpenproletarian-dominated middle ranks. As people who had been outcasts, propertyless, single, and yet had wider contact with the outside world than peasants, the lumpenproletarians had been the natural constituents of the cutting edge of the rural revolution. But as people whose lifestyles and experiences—as gamblers and smugglers, and the like—had been entirely different from the majority of the farming population, they could not as a group make ideal mass-line cadres. (From 1931 on, as I shall show in the next section, the party was to rely entirely on recruiting cadres from among activists surfacing in mass campaigns—a far better source of mass leaders than lumpenproletarians.)

It is not surprising, therefore, to find Mao criticizing the Yongfeng leadership for their high-and-mighty bureaucratic style and their dictatorial abuse of public opinion. They had, according to Mao, set themselves apart from the people, acting like mighty officials and talking to the people only when they felt like it. They had turned the new soviet government into something of an exclusive club—open to party members but not to leaders of the masses. They had made a farce of elections of deputies by simply handpicking the government personnel. They had insisted on recruiting only good-looking women for administrative work, passing over the ugly ones regardless of ability. They had even stooped to selling confiscated goods, as a favor, to those people who were well connected (Mao, 1931.1.26: 245-246). Such weaknesses in the leadership could only aggravate the problems that arose out of land reform.

At the end of 1930, therefore, the revolutionary movement in Xingguo presented a mixed picture. On the one hand, social revolution in the villages had set the preconditions for forging a genuine bond between the urban-originated movement and the peasants, the crucial link for the larger revolution to come. On the other hand, the movement was still plagued by serious weaknesses. Within the party itself, lumpenproletarians remained powerful on the county and district levels. Mao's defeat of the Futian revolt had eliminated Duan Qifeng's influence on the provincial level, but rectification of the party organization at the county and district levels had yet to begin. At the same time, the newly absorbed township and village-level cadres had yet to be trained and brought fully into the party organization. The new bonds between the party and the rural populace had yet to be reinforced and developed.

The Second Encirclement Campaign of the Guomindang, which reoccupied Xingguo in April 1931, showed how brittle some of those bonds could be. To the distress of the communists, the Guomindang commanders were able to generate some popular support for their counterrevolution. As the Communist county party committee observed, landlords and rich peasants were not the only participants; substantial numbers of the poorer villagers also joined in Guomindang-organized suppression. Some helped to identify revolutionary activists. Others took advantage of the overturn to seize the properties of sympathizers of the revolution who had run away before the Guomindang armies arrived. Still others simply looted. The result was that when the Red forces returned in June, they found a terrible mess to untangle (Xingduo xianwei, 1931.6.16). Thoroughgoing rectification of the movement was to begin only in the fall of 1931.

## The Soviet Movement

The leadership and momentum for rectification came in part from Mao and his supporters, after their triumph over Li Li-san and the Futian rebels. After the establishment of the Soviet Republic in November 1931, Mao's institutional base, as Trygve Lötviet has so ably and clearly shown, rested above all in the governmental apparatus, especially the two highest executive and legislative bodies: the Central Executive Committee and its Presidium, and the Council of People's Commissars, both of which Mao chaired (until he was replaced in the latter position by Zhang Wen-tian in February 1934) (Lötveit, 1973: 66-97).

Leadership for rectification came in part also from the newly returned group of students who had studied at the Sun Yat-sen University in Moscow. Led by Wang Ming (Chen Shao-yu—only 24 years old in 1930) and Bo Gu (Qin Bang-xian) and nicknamed the "28 Bolsheviks," they gained control over the party's central organs in Shanghai at the fourth plenum of the (sixth) Central Committee in January 1931. They were backed by the authority of the Comintern, in the person of Pavel Mif, formerly Rector of the Sun Yat-sen University. From early 1931 on, their authority was represented in the Central Soviet Area by the new Central Bureau of the Soviet Areas, until the Central Committee itself formally moved to Ruijin in early 1933 (Lötveit, 1973: 9-11, 214, 215).

Mao and the "28 Bolsheviks" agreed in important respects: in their opposition to Li Li-san and his followers, and in their shared desire to weed out the large numbers of opportunists who had been absorbed into the party during the preceding years of confusion and weakness. Both believed that mass campaigns should be the main method for purging as well as for recruiting cadres. Where they disagreed, as we shall see, was over their respective interpretations of the meaning and application of "proletarian leadership"—the "28 Bolsheviks" tended to be much more rigidly doctrinaire in their insistence that workers and workers alone should be in positions of leadership in the party and the government.[4] In the attack on Li Li-san's followers and on lumpenproletarians in the party, such as the Duan brothers, however, the two sides were in sufficient agreement to act together. Such was the background, at the level of central leadership, to the rectification campaigns in Xingguo during 1931-1934.

The overhaul of the top leadership in Xingguo began soon after the Red Army reoccupied the county in June 1931. The Central leadership seized the occasion to order, on June 17, that the old county party committee immediately turn over its work to a newly created South Jiangxi Special Committee, headed by Chen Yi (Gannan tewei, 1931.6.17).

But the work of the new committee was almost immediately interrupted by a renewed offensive (The Third Encirclement Campaign) from the Guomindang, which once more occupied Xingguo. Thorough reconstruction of the local leadership was undertaken only after September, during fifteen months of respite from Guomindang military pressure, when Chiang Kai-shek was forced to concern himself for a time more with Japanese aggression than with the communists.

The fall 1931 election of delegates to the First National Congress of Soviet Deputies (held in November 1931) provided the occasion for the first purging of local leadership through a mass election campaign. The election regulations placed more stress on class background, favoring "workers"—defined as industrial and agricultural workers, and employees and apprentices in handicrafts (Ningdu xianwei, 1932.1.18)—over all others. At the basic township level, every five workers were to elect one representative, while nonworkers elected only one representative for every fifty persons over 16 years old. Township delegates were then to elect district representatives, separately between workers and nonworkers. One intention on which Mao and the "28 Bolsheviks" could agree, was to eliminate the excessive influence of lumpenproletarians and rich peasants. As the propaganda pamphlet issued by the Xingguo county government under Chen Yi put it:

> "How are we to reconstruct our local soviet governments?" "By cleaning out. . .rich peasants, riffraff and other reactionaries, and electing good and

capable representatives of the workers, agricultural laborers, poor peasants, coolies, and honest and brave middle peasants and working women to carry out the work of the soviet." ("Guanyu guanguo suweiai daibiao dahui de wenda.")

At the same time, however, the regulations reflected a degree of prejudicial favoring of workers over poor peasants with which the rural-oriented Mao probably disagreed. A village of one hundred middle and poor peasant voters and ten agricultural workers, for example, would have elected two middle or poor peasant delegates and two agricultural workers. Such a disprportionate emphasis on agricultural workers, as Lynda Bell shows in her article in this volume, did not have any practical basis, only theoretical: they were "proletarian" in that, like the industrial proletariat, their labor had become a commodity which they sold for a living. But they did not in reality seem to have been more revolutionary or intrinsically better rural leaders than poor peasants. In any event, such heavy reliance on a group that totalled at most 5 to 10% of the rural population could hardly have been conducive to rallying the support of the majority of the villagers.

The National Congress in November formalized election regulations for subsequent campaigns and did away with excessive emphasis on "the proletariat." The new regulations distinguished, instead, simply between qualified urban and rural residents. The former was favored, at a ratio of five to one, but rural residents now cast votes equally for representatives to their township congress, without any artificial distinctions between "worker" and peasant ("Zhonghua suweiai gongheguo de xuanju xize"). The earlier regulations had been found to be unsatisfactory and this new election law governed the "Hundred Days' (December 20, 1931 to March 31, 1932) Movement to Construct the Soviets."

The intended pattern for the movement was laid out in the election law. Leadership on all levels were subjected to a reexamination process that sandwiched each level between the next higher level and the masses (or their elected representatives). Thus, the new township congress (which would choose the administrative personnel of the township from within its own ranks) was to be elected by the masses under the direction of a district level election committee. Tight guidance was ensured by requiring that all members of the district election committee be reviewed by the county government, and appointed only by the provincial government. The election committee, thus appointed, was responsible for publicizing the election and registering voters. The committee also prepared the slate of candidates, in consultation with labor unions, poor peasant corps, and other mass organizations. The final election was carried out at open mass meetings in each of the villages. Each candidate was introduced and expression of opinion from the masses was encouraged, before final election by a show of hands. Once the township soviets were constituted, the process then went upward along the govermental hierarchy. Thus township delegates elected district delegates under the direction of the county, and district delegates elected county delegates under the direction of selected provincial cadres ("Zhonghua suweiai gongheguo de xuanju xize"; "Xuanju weiyuanhui de gongzuo xize": 84-85; He, 1953: 48-49).

This process was repeated in the fall of 1932 in most counties of the Central Soviet Area. Township, district and county soviets were once more reexamined to weed out as many of the undesirable leaders as possible and to seek to generate as high a percentage of activist cadres as possible (Mao, 1932.9.20: 131-133).

Twelve months later, in the fall of 1933, local leadership was once again called into question by a third election campaign. The election regulations of August 1933 renewed the 1931 stress on "proletarian leadership" (article 3). The distinction between workers and peasants in the rural township soviets was reintroduced: there was to be one representative for every thirteen workers, as compared with one for every fifty peasants (article 21). The distinction between workers and non-workers was even extended to towns and cities: there, every twenty workers were to elect one representative, compared with one representative for every eighty of the other urban residents (article 23). The regulations further set quotas of minimum worker representation: in the district congress, 20 to 25%; county, 20 to 30%; province, 25 to 35%; national, 25 to 30% (articles 26, 27, 28, 29) ("Suweiai zhanxing xuanju fa": 309-315).

Such rigid emphasis on "proletarian" class background probably reflected the increased influence of the "28 Bolsheviks." In the "Resolutions Concerning Certain Historical Questions," Mao was to specifically criticize the group for having attacked too many of the old cadres too indiscriminately, while carelessly promoting too many new cadres (Mao, 1945 "Guanyu. . .": 986).

But, as the "Resolutions" went on to point out, the overall effect of the soviet movement was a positive one that succeeded in weeding out undesirable cadres and broadening the popular basis of the revolution. And the "28 Bolsheviks" were given credit for their part in the soviet movement (Mao, 1945 "Guanyu. . .": 974).

The evidence available on Xingguo permits only a glimpse at how all these policies translated into action. In Yongfeng district at the end of

1930, it will be recalled, outside intellectuals and local lumpenproletarians dominated the revolutionary government. By the summer of 1933, however, the class composition of the local leadership had clearly changed greatly. County-level cadres in Xingguo, as in 15 other counties (a total of 419 cadres) surveyed, came overwhelmingly from "workers" (46%) and poor peasants (44%). Most of these cadres had been recruited into the party through the land revolution and the soviet movement, rather than earlier, as the following table shows:

## TABLE I

| Year Entered Party | Number | % |
|---|---|---|
| 1927 & before | 13 | 3 |
| 1928-29 | 52 | 12 |
| 1930 | 125 | 30 |
| 1931-32 | 190 | 45 |
| 1933 | 39 | 10 |
| total | 419 | 100 |

*Source: Jiangxi shengwei, 1933.9.20*

The revolutionary movement was thus no longer an outside movement of urban intellectuals and rural outcasts, but had succeeded in drawing leaders from the farming population itself.

At the same time, there had emerged an organizational pattern through which the party reached into the villages and ensured some measure of mass participation. The basic principle was to rely on a core group of local activists through whom larger and larger numbers of people became involved in the work of the soviets, in a pattern resembling a series of widening concentric circles. Thus, the core of the township soviet was the Presidium of the township congress, which consisted of only five to seven people and met every five days. The Presidium in turn met frequently with the chairs and vice-chairs of the villages, and, every ten days, with the entire township congress. The delegates of the township congress in turn often involved nondelegates in the work of the administrative committees of the congress. They also met with their constitutencies every ten days. Finally, mass meetings of all villagers were held twice a month. The intent was to involve the largest number of people possible (Mao, 1934.4.10).

The principle that parallelled mass involvement was that of constant review of the leadership, by repeating again and again the process of selection. Thus the township congress, as we have seen, went through two re-elections in two years. And township administrative committees were reconstituted every six months. The intent was to generate constant pressure toward maximizing the proportion of activists who enjoyed genuine mass support (Mao, 1934.4.10: 349).

Once again, the evidence available permits only a glimpse at how all this translated into practice in Xingguo. In Changgang township (of Shangshe district in Xingguo), the November 1932 election (no information on the earlier election is available) identified fifty-odd delegates to the township congress, representing four villages with a total population of 1,784.[5] Of these fifty plus delegates, the political performance of 60% were assessed by Mao to have been "good," 35% "medium," and 5% "poor." Those who performed poorly (they had attended only four out of ten meetings and had not taken on any work responsibilities) were replaced in July, without waiting for the formal elections in the fall. The thirty-some "good" activists served as the core of the township government (Mao, 1933.12.15: 131-141, 151).

But this activist core, instead of becoming the basis upon which a sound soviet government could be built, was quickly drained off by the war effort. The Central Soviet Area, it must be remembered, was faced with five successive encirclement campaigns; revolutionary war had to be the greatest single preoccupation of life in the base area. The manpower needs could of course have been met by conscription, but the central leadership chose to stress voluntary enlistment. The result was that the politically activated usually became the first to enlist. In Changgang, all but two or three of the original group of male delegates elected in November 1932 had joined the war effort by the time of the 1933 elections (Mao, 1933.12.15: 131).

Such a drain placed tremendous stress on local government. Each enlistee-delegate had had to be replaced by an "acting delegate," chosen by an ad hoc election among the departing delegate's constituents. Unless the new political processes succeeded in activating increasing numbers of people, the township government would have been reduced to lesser and lesser effectiveness with each activist's departure.

Changgang was apparently able to cope with this drain without suffering a decline in the quality of its political leadership. Of the fifty-five delegates elected in November 1933, thirty-six were rated by Mao as "activists," and nineteen as "intermediate"—about the same, in other words, as the original congress (Mao, 1933.12.15: 136).

One important source of replacement for the enlisted delegates was newly activated peasant women. The efforts of the cental leadership to organize and involve women in revolution, production and war are detailed in Kathy Walker's article in this volume. Much headway was indeed made, as Walker shows. However, I believe the decisive impetus for activating peasant women came only with full-scale mobilization for war.

In Changgang, the elections of November 1932 had resulted in slightly less than 20% representation for the women (Mao, 1933.12.15: 132). Although this was certainly impressive when compared with the position women had occupied before the revolution, and, in fact, placed Changgang far ahead of other localities in the soviet area (which were to strive for a comparable proportion of female delegates only in the election in 1933) (Mao, 1933.9.6), it certainly was still a far cry from the central leadership's declared goal of liberation and fully equal participation for women.

A couple of figures for the soviet area as a whole will suffice to indicate the relative status of women in the revolutionary movement: in April 1933, women still accounted for only 11% of party members in Jiangxi province. In September 1933, women cadres totalled only 6.4% of all cadres in sixteen county governments of the soviet area (Luo Mai, 1933; Jiangxi shengwei, 1933.9.20). Full equality could not be achieved overnight, and, in spite of the declared intent of the central leadership, there must have been a great deal of resistance on the middle and lower ranks of the party, as well as among the peasant population.

The breakthrough in Changgang came only with the accelerated pace of war mobilization. Half of the original group of male delegates were enlisted in the month of May 1933 alone. An intense recruitment drive continued through the summer and fall, so that, by the time of November 1933, only eighty-seven males of the service ages of 16 to 45 were left in the township. The adult population (numbering 413 between the ages of 16 and 45) were now overwhelmingly female. Under such conditions, women came to shoulder the main burden for production. They also dominated the new elections (Mao, 1933.12.15: 151).

The contrast between village life before and after the soviet revolution was very great indeed. Villagers who had long been accustomed to associating government principally with the hateful tax collector, had become politicized in large numbers. Every peasant, if he or she were not a delegate, had at least a friend, neighbor, or relative who was active in the township soviet government. Everyone could not help but participate at least to some extent in the new postrevolutionary organizations and activities—as a member of the party, the soviets, the poor peasants' corps, the women's worker-peasant congresses, the Red Guards, the Young Pioneers, the Children's Corps, and so on; in neighborhood meetings called by the elected delegate and in village mass meetings; and, of course, in one after another mass campaigns (for production, for army recruitment, for literacy, against Guomindang subversion, and so on), especially the repeated election campaigns to construct, and then reconstruct, the village and township governments (Mao, 1933.12.15: 148-151, 154-156, 166).

Perhaps no better proof of the politicization of the Xingguo population can be offered than the report of one Lü Xian, who inspected the county for twelve days on behalf of the new Guomindang Jiangxi government in November 1934, just after the Reds had left on the Long March:

> The young men and women and children of this county have been deeply bandit-ized. They know only of the soviet and do not know of the Republic of China. They know only of the western calendar year 1934, and do not know of the twenty-third year of the Republic.

Lü complained that he could not identify any suitable people to head the *baojia* structure that the Guomindang planned to institute. The most urgent need, he concluded, was for a corps of teachers to be brought from the outside to begin the task of reeducating the population (Hatano, 1961: 724, 719-738).

The historical significance of Xingguo, of course, lies not so much in its "model" status as in what it tells us about the typical problems of the time (for models were and are chosen not because of their exemplary resolution of atypical problems, but because they show the direction for resolving *typical* problems). Driven from the cities into the countryside, radical intellectuals at first allied with the rural outcasts and outlaws—the lumpenproletariat—who served as the cutting edge of the revolution. With such a membership and without stable base areas, the party could have easily degenerated into mere roving bandits. It was only through land reform and systematic involvement of the farming population in the exercise of revolutionary power that the party was able to forge a genuine link with the countryside. That bond, between intellectuals and peasant men and women, was the key to the larger revolution to come; it was first forged in the rural base areas of the Jiangxi period.

¹This is a guess based on the information that there were about one thousand party members operating in northern Jiangxi at the end of 1926 (Smedley, 1956: 187). Organizing work was much more advanced in the Nanchang area than in southern Jiangxi.

²This sentence was later edited in the *Selected Works* to read: "There were very large numbers *(henda de shuliang)* of floating elements *(youmin chengfen)* in the Red Army" (Mao, 1929.12: 9). The English version of the *Selected Works* has rendered this as "the proportion of vagabond elements is large. . ." (Mao, 1965: I: 114).

³Mori Masao (Mori, 1975) traces the roots of these granaries to the 18th century.

⁴A good example of Wang Ming's doctrinaire stress on class origins is his views on agricultural workers, analyzed by Lynda Bell in her article in this volume.

⁵At the time of the November 1932 election, the four villages of Changgang were still a part of Langmu xiang. The information cited here has been extrapolated from that given for Langmu.

# Agricultural Laborers and Rural Revolution*
## Lynda Schaefer Bell

One goal of the Chinese Communist Party from its founding was to develop proletarian leadership for the Chinese revolution. As members of a political party working for socialism, Chinese communists considered this an essential component of their revolutionary program. Beginning in 1927, however, the party's efforts to develop mass support for the revolution were largely confined to the countryside. One question they faced, therefore, was how to meet their original goal of proletarian leadership and socialist revolution, while simultaneously working to mobilize the rural population for revolutionary struggle. A method suggested by top-ranking party leaders beginning in 1928 was to rely on agricultural laborers as rural proletarians to provide leadership for the movement. This paper examines the development of this idea, its failure to take root in rural work, and new, successful solutions which the party began to formulate by 1934, to the fundamental problems of rural mass mobilization and the meaning of proletarian leadership in the Chinese context.

### The Rural Proletariat

Agricultural laborers were those people in Chinese rural society who owned virtually no land or farming implements and who made their living wholly or mainly by selling their labor power (Mao, 1933.6).[1] In addition to male workers, there were also women and children who fit this category (Smedley, 1936: 54-55). Rich peasants, the main employers of agricultural labor, often employed one or several workers on a long-term, annual basis (Mao, 1933.6). But there were also those who worked only seasonally, monthly, or daily to assist in planting and harvesting (Lee, 1951: 239-241; Liu, 1951: 47). These short-term workers sometimes migrated from place to place, but often remained in one location where

*Author's note: I would like to thank Ed Hammond, Trygve Lötveit, and Dennis Engbarth for their comments on an earlier draft of this article.

they worked as coolies, peddlars, or manure and firewood gatherers for part of each year (Lee, 1951: 241; Wang Yu-quan, 1935: 2-3). Agricultural laborers who could find little or no work on a regular basis were eventually pushed out of rural production altogether, becoming bandits or wandering beggars—an indication of their precarious position in rural society. It was very rare indeed that an agricultural laborer was able to move upward in social or economic status (Lee, 1951: 243-245).

Working singly or in small groups on fragmented plots rented or privately owned by other peasants, agricultural laborers were widely scattered throughout the countryside. Large-scale farming enterprises, employing many workers in one location, did not exist in early twentieth-century China (Wang Yu-quan, 1935: 1-2). Dispersed working conditions, coupled with the transitory nature of short-term work, made it very difficult to calculate the total number of hired workers (Lee, 1951: 238-239).

The most widely used estimate has been that agricultural laborers made up approximately 10% of China's total rural population (Chen, 1935: 58). Unfortunately, the sampling method used by the researcher who arrived at this figure was poor, and his sample limited in size.[2] Both long and short-term laborers, as well as some poor peasants who worked for wages only seasonally, were included in his estimate. Therefore, the number of people who could strictly be called agricultural laborers was almost certainly less than 10%. To corroborate this view, at least for Jiangxi province, field workers there in 1951 found that in areas not yet affected by land reform (and therefore likely to have a high percentage of hired workers relative to other areas), agricultural laborers made up only 3.7% of the rural population (Liu, 1951: 43). Even if both long and short-term workers were classified as agricultural laborers by party cadres working in the countryside (as was very likely the case—see Mao, 1931.1.26: 199, 222), they were still only a small minority of the total rural population.

Despite indications that agricultural laborers were relatively few in number and difficult to identify as a distinct group, many Communist Party members stressed their unique position in rural society in the late 1920s as exploited wage laborers. Owning none of the means of production or subsistence themselves, agricultural laborers were, in this somewhat limited sense at least, the rural proletariat. Thus they were viewed by some as potential leaders of the rural movement.

Many policies stressing the leading role of agricultural laborers were suggested for implementation in the soviet areas in the early 1930s. Important party leaders of urban intellectual background, having no experience as yet in rural work, were responsible for this trend in policy-making for the rural movement. They developed an analysis of the Chinese revolution throughout this period which pointed to the development of capitalism in rural China, and hence, stressed the speed with which socialism could be established (Mao, 1945 "Resolutions...": 181). In their view, these two issues were intimately linked—without rural capitalism and leadership of a rural proletariat, there could be no rural revolution which could quickly provide a socialist conclusion. Indeed, at times their argument came close to suggesting that without these factors, there could be no rural revolution at all.

As it related to rural class structure, their analysis acknowledged that feudal landlord-peasant relationships were still prevalent, but stressed also that new capitalist class relations in the countryside were developing very rapidly. Thus, the struggle that grew out of more advanced capitalist relations, between agricultural laborers on the one hand and rich peasants, their employers, on the other, would become one essential focal point of the rural revolution. Out of this struggle would come the proletarian leadership necessary to lead the rural movement as rapidly as possible through its bourgeois-democratic phase (land equalization) into a period of socialist revolution (nationalization of land and collectivized production). The result of this analysis was their effort to identify and put into positions of political power a group of rural proletarians in the Chinese countryside, where feudal landlord-poor peasant antagonisms were actually the principal problem.[3]

The trend to concentrate on agricultural laborers as proletarian leaders began under the leadership of Qu Qiu-bai and Li Li-san from 1928 to 1930, but reached its apex in the period 1931 to 1934, through the influence of Wang Ming and the 28 Bolsheviks. Recently returned from study at the Comintern-run Sun Yat-sen University in Moscow, Wang Ming and his supporters were expert theoreticians but lacked concrete information about conditions in rural China. They remained in Shanghai for the most part, the base of the party Central Committee, until late 1932 or early 1933.[4] Wang Ming himself probably never travelled to the Central Soviet Area, remaining in Shanghai to work for the party publication *Red Flag* (Hongqi), and serving briefly as secretary-general of the party from June through August 1931 (Sheng, 1971: 235, 245-246). He went to Moscow in September 1931, as the head of the Chinese delegation to the Comintern, and did not return again to China until 1937 (Sheng, 1971: 246). Nevertheless, it was primarily under Wang Ming's influence on party policy-making that a distorted analysis of the agricultural laborer question and its relationship to proletarian leadership of the rural revolution developed.

## Party Leaders and Agricultural Laborers, 1928-1930

At the Sixth Congress of the Chinese Communist Party, held in Moscow in June and July of 1928 (Grigor'ev, 1975: 28; Sheng, 1971: 191-199), both Qu Qiu-bai, current secretary-general of the party, and Li Li-san advanced the position that agricultural laborers, as the rural proletariat, should become the foundation of leadership for the revolution in the countryside. In a discussion of rural class relations at the Congress, Qu devoted his attention to defining rich peasants as capitalists, no different from factory owners who exploit hired labor, and agricultural laborers as the rural proletariat (Deliusin, 1975: 83-84). Like Qu, Li Li-san also stressed the fact that capitalism in the countryside was emerging alongside of the existing system of feudal exploitation and claimed that "the peasant masses are being exploited and proletarianized." He claimed that "Large-scale capitalist production is born as a result of this process" (Deliusin, 1975: 79). He opposed egalitarian division of the land because it would lead to the further development of capitalism. The common thread that ran through Qu and Li's assertions was that only socialism could solve China's agricultural problems; therefore, the bourgeois-democratic revolution had to be completed by relying on the leadership of the rural proletariat and socialism had to be established very rapidly. One method Li and others at the Congress recommended for accelerating the process was to organize agricultural laborers into unions separate from other peasant organizations to prepare them for their ensuing struggle against rich peasants (Deliusin, 1975: 80-81, 90). As we shall see, this was an idea later taken up and thoroughly developed by Wang Ming for application in the soviet areas.

In the course of the debates on these issues, other delegates at the Congress stated that, in their view, capitalism was *not* developed to any great degree in the countryside, and pointed out that there were actually very few rich peasants or agricultural laborers (Deliusin, 1975: 86, 94). The final resolutions of the Congress on the agrarian and peasant questions, however, virtually ignored this view. "Resolution on the Agrarian Question," in its description of the social structure of the countryside, insisted that "the army of agricultural proletarians is forming" (Deliusin, 1975:93); thus the essential struggle in the countryside would develop not between landlords on the one hand and peasants on the other, but rather, between the rural bourgeoisie and the rural proletariat (Deliusin, 1975: 95).

Other resolutions of the Congress also took this position and developed it further.

"Resolution on the Land Question" defined agricultural laborers as the rural proletariat and rich peasants, their employers, as the rural bourgeoisie. In this formulation, agricultural laborers were considered comparable to their wage-labor counterparts in cities, the industrial proletariat, and were viewed as potential leaders of the rural revolution (Zhongguo gongchandang diliuci, 1928.7). "Resolution on the Peasant Movement" devoted an entire section to defining the role of the rural proletariat, calling for the establishment of independent organizations of agricultural laborers in areas where a "rich peasant economy" already existed, and for cells of agricultural laborers to be set up within peasant associations in other areas. In this way, the leadership role of agricultural laborers would be strengthened. Furthermore, a liaison was to be established between these organizations and workers' unions at the county-level. The intention was to develop the movement of workers in both city and countryside in order to provide strong proletarian leadership for the agrarian revolution (Zhongguo gongchandang diliuci, 1928.9).

In keeping with the view that agricultural laborers were the rural proletariat with a special role to play, was a desire to institute measures ensuring that they would retain that position in rural society during the phase of bourgeois-democratic revolution. Translated into policy-making, this meant that to avoid transforming agricultural laborers into small-scale farmers, they should not be given land in the process of land confiscation and distribution; if they had already received land, they should pool that land to make collective farms. Li Li-san presented no consistent position on this issue at the Sixth Party Congress, although he did suggest at one point that agricultural laborers should receive no land at all (Deliusin, 1975: 90). In the two years following the Congress, however, Li developed this idea in conjunction with his stand that immediate socialism through nationalization of land rather than land equalization was the only proper remedy for the ills of the countryside. This was one point against which Wang Ming's forces and the Comintern allied when all of Li's policies were called into question beginning in mid-1930.

### Wang Ming, the Comintern, and Agricultural Laborer Unions

In 1930-31, while the Central Committee was still located in Shanghai, the party organ *Red Flag* was used to circulate Central Committee views throughout the entire party membership. Although various Central Committee members and their urban-based colleagues may have lacked first-hand knowledge in many instances on base area conditions, there was little reluctance on their part to offer opinions on matters of soviet organization and revolutionary activity in general. On his return from Moscow in 1930, Wang Ming began to write for *Red Flag* and also began his rise within the party hierarchy. As already noted, in June 1931, at age 25, he became acting secretary-general of the party for a brief period. After this, he continued his influence by becoming the primary liaison between the Comintern and the Chinese party (Rue, 1966: 239-255).

In May 1930, a series of three articles by Wang Ming appeared in *Red Flag* entitled, "Why Are We Not Organizing Agricultural Laborer Unions?", and was subtitled, "Peasant Mentality, Especially Rich Peasant Mentality, is the Culprit" (Wang Ming, 1930). Wang Ming's basic theme was that in the countryside, especially in the newly forming soviet base areas, the party's primary task was to organize unions composed solely of agricultural laborers. It was important that only the agricultural laborers, the hired wage earners, be allowed to join these groups. According to Wang Ming, only through this type of "independent class organization" could the party hope to build a successful rural revolutionary base. Class distinctions in the rural areas had to be made clear, and organizational policy formulated by strictly adhering to the idea of proletarian leadership for the revolution.

Apparently, some party members had been raising doubts and questions about this proposed tactic for mass organizing activity. Wang Ming felt that these comrades were victims of what he called "rich peasant capitalist mentality." For him, this meant that they failed to understand that party work in the countryside should concentrate even during land reform on eliminating the peasants' desire to own a private share of land and to work only in their own self interest. Rich peasants embodied this small-peasant-producer attitude in its highest form because they were the most successful in realizing its goal. Agricultural laborers were the only group in the countryside, in Wang Ming's estimation, that could work against this tendency because they were the only ones who neither owned nor rented any land of their own. In Wang Ming's view, then, only if the party worked to organize agricultural laborers into unions to fight against rich peasants could it become a true party of the proletariat. In his words:

> A question must be seriously and clearly raised in the following way: Are we afraid of rich peasant opposition and therefore fail to organize agricultural laborers? Well then, we are certainly not the political party of the proletariat!

Alternatively, we may say: If we *are* the political party of the proletariat, then we must make a special effort to organize agricultural laborers to oppose rich peasants! (1930.5.24.)

At the end of the series, Wang Ming summed up his position as follows:

Under the present situation of rapid revolutionary development, and under conditions in which the class struggle is being broadened and deepened, when the question of revolutionary transformation has already become an urgent one for us, the question of organizing agricultural laborer unions (of equal importance in both soviet areas and non-soviet areas) truly occupies an exceptionally serious position! Rural party organizations and urban red labor union organizations must initiate a most determined and strong effort to organize and lead the most undeveloped, bleakest, bitterest, and most unorganized struggles of the rural proletariat; establish, expand and consolidate their independent class organizations; and make them not only a vanguard to realize the completion of the bourgeois-democratic revolution but also a rural "pillar" to bring about the revolutionary transformation to socialism and to realize the victory of the dictatorship of the proletariat! (1930.5.24)

Thus, Wang Ming believed that if the proletarian leadership potential of agricultural laborers was realized through agricultural laborer unions, the transition to socialism could come about in China very quickly. Supposedly, this was different from thinking that the bourgeois-democratic revolution could be passed over entirely, the error attributed by Wang Ming and the Comintern throughout late 1930 and 1931 to Li Li-san. Rather, Wang Ming's position was that under proletarian leadership of agricultural laborer unions, the rich peasants' ability to develop capitalism in the countryside would be significantly curbed, and the stages of revolution compressed. In this formulation, land equalization was to be a necessary, but brief, stage.

Despite Wang Ming's consistent criticism of Li Li-san's position on agricultural laborers and immediate collectivization, his own position, as we shall see, was to have much the same impact on the rural movement—effectively limiting broad expansion of organizing efforts among the rural population and hence, also on the anti-feudal movement for land reform. In fact, because Wang Ming was able to use sophisticated theoretical arguments and to quote from Marxist classics to build his argument that agricultural laborer unions would pave the way for the dictatorship of the proletariat, his position was much more difficult to oppose than Li's had been and had much more influence within the Central Committee. In addition, he had Cominten support (Mao, 1945 "Resolutions. . .": 182).

Late in 1930, the Comintern dealt specifically with the issue of immediate collectivization and the failure to allow agricultural laborers to keep land, blaming Li Li-san for causing such problems. They stated that proposals made in some places for agricultural laborers to combine the land they had received in the initial confiscation and redistribution process to make "soviet farms" had been symptoms of Li Li-san's left deviation (Gongchan guoji dongfangbu, 1930.11.20).

The Comintern-Wang Ming forces consolidated their criticism of Li Li-san's position on agricultural laborers and collectivization early in 1931. At that time, both the Comintern and Wang Ming's views were reflected in the work of the Central Bureau of the Soviet Areas, established in January of that year to represent the Central Committee within the base areas. Early in 1931, the Central Bureau pointed out that collectivization of land in Soviet Russia had been delayed for more than ten years after the initial outbreak of the revolution, and hence was not appropriate at this early stage of the rural movement in China. Annihilation of Chinese rich peasants, the opponents of collectivization and the enemies of agricultural laborers, was not the proper goal at this stage either (as it was viewed in Russia during this period), but rather, strict curbing of their political influence and economic exploitation (Zhonggong suqu zhongyangju, 1931.2.8).

As an alternative to immediate collectivization to combat the interests of rich peasants and to promote the political role of agricultural laborers, the Comintern suggested the establishment of independent class organizations of the rural proletariat—namely, agricultural laborer unions (Gongchan guoji dongfangbu, 1930.11.20; Guoji, 1931.2.18). Based on information provided by Wang Ming as the new head of the Comintern Chinese delegation, Li Li-san was again blamed for suggestions raised in many areas to forego completely the distribution of land to agricultural laborers, on the basis that they should be building collective farms instead. Wang Ming also stated that in the wake of Li Li-san's defeated position, hundreds of thousands of agricultural laborers had already become members of agricultural laborer unions and that this was a matter of the greatest importance in the Chinese labor movement, the land revolution, and the struggle to establish soviets (Guoji gunong weiyuanhui mishuchu, 1931.12 [?]).

Later evidence will make it clear that this was an enormous overstatement on Wang Ming's part of the success of organizing efforts among rural workers. But at this point in the rural movement, both he and the Comintern had put their hopes for its future growth in realizing the independent political role of agricultural laborers as the rural proletariat, through the vehicle of agricultural laborer unions.

Within the Chinese party leadership, others were following the Comintern-Wang Ming lead. For example, another article appeared in *Red Flag* in May 1930, arguing precisely the same points concerning agricultural laborer unions. This article, entitled "How to Oppose Rich Peasants," was written by Ruan Xiao-xian, an activist from the earlier peasant movement in Guangdong, and director of the third session of the Peasant Training Institute in Canton [Guangzhou] in 1925. Among the seven points outlined, one stressed that agricultural laborers must be independently organized for class struggle against rich peasants. It was the party's duty to explain that agricultural laborers and the rural bourgeoisie, rich peasants, were mutually opposed. Developing the leadership of agricultural laborers was the basic work of the party in the villages in order to liquidate the rich peasant line. This task was to be taken up as the most urgent responsibility of each village cell (Ruan, 1930).

Subsequently, two articles appeared in *Red Flag* in June 1930, written under the pen name Chang Han,[5] concerning work among agricultural laborers in Wanxian, a county very near Baoding city, center of revolutionary work in southern Hebei. Linda Grove has recently demonstrated that the work radiating from that center during 1932, based on regular contacts between the Hebei party committee and the Shanghai-based Central Committee, led to serious mistakes in military strategy, in this case an armed uprising which led to the eventual defeat of the Gaoyang-Lixian Soviet established near Baoding (Grove, 1975). Adventurism in military matters, calling for armed uprisings in towns and cities when little groundwork had been laid for the establishment of revolutionary control afterwards, was the single most serious problem resulting from the advice of the Central Committee at this time. But military strategy was not their only field of influence. By putting forward in *Red Flag* the case of organizing agricultural laborers in Wanxian as an example for others to follow, the Central Committee was defining mass organizing among agricultural laborers as another important area in which it wanted others to act. It is not surprising that one of the examples of revolutionary activity prior to the establishment of the Gaoyang-Lixian Soviet was a struggle centering around the issue of low wages received by hired laborers (Grove, 1975: 247).

In the *Red Flag* articles on Wanxian, the plea was made once again for the establishment both at the village and county-wide levels of independent agricultural laborer unions. Demands of agricultural laborers in Wanxian such as increased wages, shorter working hours, equal pay for equal work for male and female workers, as well as examples of improvements in their conditions based on specific struggles, were presented. In this way, an important foundation was to be laid on which to build soviet political power (Chang Han, 1930a; 1930b). Thus, as a result of the analysis advanced by Wang Ming and implemented by his 28 Bolshevik supporters working within the Central Committee, work among agricultural laborers had become the focal point of mass organizing efforts in Wanxian. It was their intention to influence other party cadres to work in a similar manner.

## Proletarian Policies in the Southern Soviet Areas

The emphasis on organizing agricultural laborers may have begun as a localized phenomenon in counties such as Wanxian, but gradually it began to permeate local work at all levels and in many places. "Provisional Regulations for the Agricultural Laborer Union," published in February 1931, called for a hierarchical structure of union organization within the soviet areas, ranging from the local level up to the provincial level. Within each province, administrative units in rural China were as follows: first, the county *(xian)*, then the district *(qu)*, next the township *(xiang)*, and finally the village *(cun)*. Within each unit, there were several progressively lower subdivisions: each county had several districts; each district, several townships; each township, several villages. There was to be an agricultural laborer union organization at each of these levels:

> Three or more members can become an agricultural laborer union small group; the members of three or more of these small groups can become an agricultural laborer union branch; three or more of these branches can become a district-level agricultural laborer union. Three or more district-level agricultural laborer unions can become a county-level agricultural laborer union. Three or more county-level agricultural laborer unions can become a provincial agricultural laborer union or a soviet special-area agricultural laborer union (Zhonghua suweiai quyu, 1931.2a).

Mass participation beginning with the village as the basic unit seems to have been the goal of the proposed organizational plan. It is worth noting, however, that the small number of members required to make an organization was an indication of how few agricultural laborers there really were.

There was also to be a congress of delegates and an all-member congress, each of which were to meet at least every three months. The representatives to the congress of delegates were to be elected once a year in proportion to the number of members in the union. It was not made clear, however, how the election procedure was actually to function. The designated work plan of the union was equally vague. An executive committee was to be appointed either by the congress of delegates or the all-member congress, and work committees set up under its jurisdiction. These were to be a department of organization, a department of propaganda, a secretariat, a committee on education, and a committee on financial matters. The struggles to be carried out under this committee structure were the traditional kinds of fights carried on by union organizations: struggles for better wages, resistance of exploitation and oppression, and the setting up of schools and clubs for the workers. No mention was made of how the union was to function in land reform—the primary work of the rural revolution. Nothing was said about land classification, confiscation or redistribution. At best, this document was a rudimentary outline of an organization through which revolutionary activists could be identified and mobilized, but provided no real guidance as to how revolutionary work was to be carried on once the union organization was established.

"Regulations for the Poor Peasant Association" was also issued within the soviet areas in February 1931. Proletarian supervision of the associations was assured by the stipulation that only on the recommendation of a worker could poor peasants be admitted to association membership. In addition, while a hierarchical organization scheme was proposed, similar to that of the agricultural laborer union, it was to go no higher than the district-level. Only three levels of organization were called for: three village poor peasant associations could become a township poor peasant association; three township poor peasant associations could become a district poor peasant association. No poor peasant associations were to be organized from the district-level on, and their work was to be closely supervised by the soviet government. This limitation on the scope of the poor peasant association was another way of assuring that the more important work of organizing agricultural laborer unions would come first, and that proletarian leadership at the higher levels would not be diluted (Zhonghua suweiai quyu, 1931.2b).

This last point was elaborated upon in "How to Organize the Poor Peasant Association and Its Tasks," probably issued also in 1931, shortly after the above two sets of regulations. It cut back the organizational scope of the poor peasant association even further, insisting that no associations were needed even at the district-level. "Small groups" of poor peasants and agricultural laborers were to be established below the township-level. But of the two kinds of groups, the agricultural laborer "small group" was to play the leading role in the association. Previously there had been a call for a systematic organization of poor peasant associations at every level. This had caused confusion by denying "the working class leadership in the Chinese revolution." The final stipulation to guarantee the principle of proletarian leadership for the rural revolution was that the chairman of the township poor peasant association had to be an agricultural laborer (Zhonggong Gan xi-nan, n.d.,

1931 [?]).

Obviously, the Wang Ming-Comintern stress on agricultural laborers as the proletarian vanguard influenced both party and government committees who made policy for the soviet areas early in 1931. Justification for identifying agricultural laborers as proletarian leaders and limiting the role of poor peasant associations was also given on the basis of practical problems relating to previous leadership developed at the local level. Rich peasants, for example, were causing many problems in soviet work. In places where remnants of old peasant associations from the 1920s existed, the old leadership, often rich peasants, still remained. In some places, rich peasants had actually been able to convince people to stop their demands for land confiscation and redistribution (Zhonggong Gan xi-nan, n.d., 1931 [?]). To overcome this problem, the plan was to hold elections or mass meetings in which agricultural laborers would replace rich peasants in positions of leadership within the associations (Guoji, 1931.2.18).

Other practical problems relating to the development of better leadership at the local level centered on minimizing the role of people who were self-employed, such as independent artisans, local Daoist monks, and village geomancers, who had joined and subsequently caused problems within agricultural laborer unions (Zhonggong suqu zhongyangju, 1931.11). We may speculate that these people had much the same effect as rich peasants by influencing the majority of poor and middle peasants to act in ways that were not necessarily in their best interests. They also had the tendency to become the tools of political manipulation on the part of rich peasants and landlords (see Philip Huang's article in this volume on the negative influence of such individuals in Xingguo county).

So the call went out consistently in 1931 and 1932 to establish new agricultural laborer unions throughout the soviet areas. Typical of the kind of action called for was a resolution of December 1931, that before April of the following year, agricultural laborer unions at all levels, as well as the provincial agricultural laborer union, were to be organized (Zhonggong Jiangxi suqu shengwei, 1931.12). By September 1932, the Hubei-Hunan-Jiangxi Provincial Agricultural Laborer Union had been established, and it put forth another call for continued growth. Those areas which had not yet established representative congress systems of agricultural laborer unions were to do so by November 15; the membership of agricultural laborer unions was to be expanded by 2,500 within the period of half a month (Hara Masaru, 1935). One example of local work was Donggu county where there was to be a systematic establishment of agricultural laborer unions and a quota of agricultural laborers on all committees, to be elected by the unions (Hara Masaru, 1935). Thus, agricultural laborer unions which were strictly independent of other classes, as well as poor peasant associations which were assured of agricultural laborer leadership, were the means set under Wang Ming's guidance to guarantee a central core of leadership of proper class background for the rural revolution.

**Rural Investigation**

While Wang Ming's distant influence was clearly felt in the southern soviet areas, Mao Ze-dong was personally responsible for several rural surveys of conditions within the base areas in 1930. In his "Investigation of Xingguo," the situation of agricultural laborers in Xingguo county's Yongfeng district was assessed (Mao, 1931.1.26).[6] Intial land redistribution had taken place in Xingguo in March 1930. Thus, it was possible to compare the position of agricultural laborers in rural society prior to and following revolutionary activity.

Clearly, agricultural laborers were among the most oppressed and exploited people in rural society. The story of Zhu Da-xi who worked on a long-term basis for a rich peasant family, confirmed this fact. There were seven people in his family—four brothers, their father, mother, and Da-xi's wife. Da-xi and the next eldest brother were both able to find work, but their total combined yearly income was only 49 *yuan*. With this money, they could buy slightly more than 16 *dan* of grain a year, but this was only enough to feed two and a half people. Thus the family relied on any other means they could just to feed themselves. The two women cut straw to make a little extra money; in winter, they only ate two meals per day; and they had borrowed money amounting to more than 30 yuan. Da-xi had no house of his own, so he lived in the stables of his employer.

In general in Yongfeng district, even when one could find a job, the terms of employment for agricultural laborers were very difficult. Working hours were long—at least ten hours a day. In the winter, when people could not work in the fields in the evenings, they had to cut wood and grind sweet potatoes for their employers. When agricultural laborers got sick, they had to buy their own medicine, and if they were sick for more than three days, their wages were cut accordingly.

One of the worst hardships for agricultural laborers had been that practically none of them had been able to afford to get married in the past. Because of this, Mao called them "the most miserable class" in the village. Even after the soviet government declared that marriages no longer had to be arranged or paid for, agricultural laborers still could not find partners. It was well known that agricultural laborers had never been able to afford tools or other household necessities and that they had never had any time to spend at home. Therefore, women of other classes were still unwilling to marry male agricultural laborers.

When they received land through the process of land confiscation and redistribution, it was still difficult for agricultural laborers to do a good job of working their own land. They had no access to work animals or agricultural tools. The soviet government had confiscated many animals and tools from landlords and rich peasants, but instead of distributing them to the agricultural laborers they had sold them.

As for the political role of the agricultural laborers, a few sentences seemed to sum it up:

> After the revolution, the agricultural laborers have not taken power politically. The middle peasants and poor peasants generally say that the agricultural laborers "know no characters, cannot speak, are not open, do not know how to handle public affairs." Therefore, they can do nothing. Among the committee people of the district and township governments of this district, there is not a single agricultural laborer. There is only one agricultural laborer who has become a captain of a Red Guard Squad (Mao, 1931.1.26: 225).

The revolution may have come to Xingguo, but agricultural laborers had not played a leading role. Moreover, it is likely that the isolation of agricultural laborers in the village was a phenomenon that existed long before the revolution began, which had its source in the nature of their working conditions.

Mao's report went on to say, for example, that in the entire district of 8,800 people, only the equivalent of 15 full-time agricultural laborers were hired each year. There may have been more than 15 individuals involved, with some people working only part-time or seasonally, but this was not made explicit in the report. Moreover, the full-time workers were dispersed widely, hired by several families. They lived with the family for whom they worked, and probably were not able to interact much with other villagers. Another report made during land reform in the early 1950s confirmed that in Jiangxi generally, the hiring of agricultural laborers was minimal and the workers scattered (Liu, 1951). Given these facts, independent class organizations in which only they participated, could only have served to further isolate them from the movement.

Mao himself draws no conclusion in his report from his observations of the isolation of agricultural laborers in Xingguo's Yongfeng district. Party members generally, however, seemed to be struggling desperately to organize agricultural laborers independently and were encountering many problems. The Secretariat of the Comintern Agricultural Labor Committee candidly stated that one source of difficulties in organizing agricultural laborer unions in China lay in "the nature of the work of the agricultural laborer." Agricultural laborers were "spread out," and their work was not stable. Many were hired yearly, but some only seasonally, monthly, or daily, and therefore, drifted from place to place. Because of this it was difficult at times just to locate the people who should join the unions (Guoji gunong weiyuanhui mishuchu, 1931.12 [?]).

Likewise, local reports from other counties in the Central Soviet Area mentioned many specific problems in organizing agricultural laborer unions. For example, in Taihe county in 1930, the soviet government had not yet established agricultural laborer unions as independent organizations and agricultural laborers had not been brought forth to participate in political power (Taihe xian gongnongbing, 1930.9.2). A subsequent report from Taihe, dated April 1931, indicated that unions there had still not become class organizations—that non-working class elements were still present. As a result, the assessment was that the unions' leadership function had not been consolidated in all revolutionary struggles (Taihe xian chise, 1931.4.26).

Another report of failure at agricultural laborer union work came from Ningdu county in mid-1932. The party and newly established soviet governments were performing most of the revolutionary work in Ningdu. Mass organizations had not been mobilized, "especially unions and agricultural laborer unions. Their leadership function had not been raised" (Zhonggong suqu zhongyangju zuzhibu, 1932.9.10).

The most striking indication that independently organizing agricultural laborers was failing to become a vital aspect of soviet work came via two reports by Mao in 1933, on work in model townships within the Central Soviet Area. Investigations were made of Changgang and Caixi townships because the soviet work in both places had been exemplary. Thus, they were considered model examples for other areas to emulate. In neither report was any mention made of agricultural laborer unions; rather, Mao called attention to the poor peasant corps. The conclusion to be drawn is that agricultural laborer unions had not been important in the process of revoluton within either of those townships (Mao, 1933.12.15; Mao, 1933; Kim, 1973: 17).

Finally, one additional glimpse into rural investigation is available to us in the form of a questionnaire used for members of rural workers' unions. In answer to the question, "What local struggles and political activity have you participated in?", one individual merely answered, "I beat up landlords." He had not joined the party or youth league in his locality, had never participated in any other political party, and had taken no responsibility for any union work (Zhongguo nongye gongren, n.d.). Unfortunately, only this one questionnaire has been located and we cannot make any very sound conclusions on the basis of this one example.

However, in conjunction with Mao's rather pessimistic appraisal of the participation of agricultural laborers in the initial revolutionary process in Xingguo, and the reports from other localities concerning the failures and difficulties in organizing agricultural laborers, this one piece of further documentation adds to the picture of minimal success in mass work through the approach of proletarian leadership based on agricultural laborer unions. Furthermore, Mao's failure to discuss such unions in any of his reports indicates his disagreement with Wang Ming's position. In Mao's view, those organizations were neither the best means to mobilize the rural population nor to develop proletarian leadership for the revolution.

**Quotas**

In 1931, another approach for involving people with proletarian class background in revolutionary work began to take shape. "Resolutions on the Soviet Areas' Labor Union Movement," a document prepared by the Central Bureau of the Soviet Areas for the First Soviet Areas' Party Congress in November 1931, proclaimed that the goal of the union movement was to link up the struggle for the interests of the laboring class with victory for the whole soviet movement (that is, building new political structures in the rural areas and developing new, activist leadership). Pure economism—limiting the union movement to seeking higher wages and better working conditions—had been a mistake of the past. Workers had not been made aware that there were larger goals of ensuring the consolidation and expansion of the entire soviet movement at stake. Thus, it was the duty of the party to rectify this situation by making union work and party work one and the same. According to the Central Bureau directive, party branches made up entirely of working class people were to be created. In this way, work within the unions could be led by party members who were also workers themselves. A new phrase was used to describe the people who should be recruited for these party branches—*gongren-gunong-kuli*—workers-agricultural laborers-coolies. In effect, a new policy of recruitment was now called for that would give the party a quota of members who came from working class backgrounds. The phrase gongren-gunong-kuli, often abbreviated gong-gu-ku, began to appear frequently in party documents, always in the context of creating a quota of people from this group for many kinds of revolutionary tasks. This document also called for setting up special training classes for new working class cadres so that they could be made into "the most realiable leadership in the eyes of the masses" (Zhonggong suqu zhongyangju, 1931.11). In order to assess what impact this new policy might have had in terms of recruitment of a larger number of people into the revolutionary movement, we must examine the size and composition of this new group of workers that the party was now dicussing.

Figures reported at the Second National Congress of Soviet Deputies by Mao Ze-dong in January 1934 indicated that there were 229,000 members of all kinds of union organizations throughout the soviet areas, and that this number was 95% of the total number of workers (Mao, 1934.1.24/25). Workers included both the "industrial proletariat"—factory workers, workers in shipping, railroads, and mines—as well as handicraft workers who owned no tools themselves, but were hired as wage-laborers by others (Zhonggong Ningdu xianwei, 1932.1.18). This entire group was less than 3% of the population of the soviet areas, with the total population approaching 9,000,000 (Snow, 1938: 92).[7] Even if they were properly trained as party cadres after initial recruitment, workers were still a very small number in the total context of Chinese rural society.

In view of the fact that there were so few workers, rigid application of quota guidelines for the gong-gu-ku alone would actually have led to minimal expansion of the soviet movement. Thus, we find in practice, that two trends in recruitment policies developed. One favored strict adherence to the worker quota ideal. The other also favored the concept of recruitment quotas, but included poor peasants, middle peasants and women, in addition to workers, in proposed quota guidelines. It is difficult to say with absolute certainty that the 28 Bolsheviks, working through the Central Bureau within the soviet areas, were responsible for the first trend, and that it was Mao's less dogmatic approach toward mass involvement which generated the second. But writing in 1945, Mao condemned the tendency to have "over-stressed the importance of the working-class origin of leading cadres to the exclusion of other considerations." Mao emphasized instead, the importance of party members becoming "proletarianized in ideology," a concept to which we shall later return (Mao, 1945 "Resolutions...": 176, 212). On this basis, I interpret the evolution of the two opposing viewpoints on quotas to be a reflection of this difference between Wang Ming and Mao on how best to achieve and develop correct leadership for the rural movement.

There are several examples of quota policies proposed during 1932 and 1933 which illustrate the development of the two opposing trends. Just one month following the Central Bureau's proposal to put emphasis on the gong-gu-ku, a document issued by the Jiangxi Soviet Area Provincial Party Committee urged a slightly different policy—that party recruitment proceed among the gong-gu-ku, but that poor peasants and the best people from among the middle peasants should also be absorbed (Zhonggong Jiangxi suqu shengwei, 1931.12). In June 1932, seven months after the gong-gu-ku policy was first proposed, 1/3 party membership from the gong-gu-ku group was still put forward as an ideal, but 1/5 of new members were also to be women (Zhonggong suqu zhongyangju zuzhibu, 1932.6.12). In terms of army recruitment, the gong-gu-ku policy was clearly insufficient to achieve necessary expansion. In the three months of July, August, and September 1932, the goal for new proletarian recruits—agricultural laborers and workers—was 33%, but it had not yet been achieved. Army membership was still only 24% proletarian (Deng, 1933).[8]

By 1933, on the eve of the Second All-Provincial Party Congress, party membership in Jiangxi had indeed skyrocketed. In one year, membership had grown from 30,000 to 97,451. But this expansion seems to have resulted almost in spite of the gong-gu-ku quota. Again, the goal of 1/3 membership from the group was proposed, but actually, in April, only 23% of new party members were from this category; in May, 28%. The new importance attached to the role of women and poor peasants was certainly more significant for continuing, long-term expansion. New membership in May had been over 20% women, a figure which corresponded to the party's stated female quota. The new goals to strive for were 100% increase in total party membership, still trying for 30% from the gong-gu-ku group, but linked with a call for a 150% increase in the number of women. Of 419 county-level cadres, it was stated that 46% were workers, but also that 44% were poor peasants (Jiangxi shengwei, 1933.9.20).

Still more recruitment campaigns seemed to proceed quite well without strict adherence to the gong-gu-ku quota policy. In June 1932, each of the 13 districts in Ningdu county, plus Ningdu city, had set quotas for increasing both party members and army members "a hundredfold," with no mention made of gong-gu-ku. The method for achieving this for party membership was simply for each party member to introduce a new member, and for every township to set up its own party branch (Ningdu xianwei, 1932.6.10).

By July, the Ningdu Party Committee was still emphasizing new party and army recruitment, but specifically including people other than the gong-gu-ku in its efforts. One goal set was "to strengthen and expand the army a hundredfold, bringing the gong-gu-ku as well as the most determined poor peasant cadres into the Red Army." As for the party, the three-month work plan for July, August, and September sent down by the Central Committee and the Provincial Committee, was to be completed by doubling party membership. 30% was to be from the gong-gu-ku group, but 15% was also to be "laboring women" (Ningdu zhongxin xianwei, 1932.7.10).

Fluctuations in the use of workers' quotas as a means to assure proletarian leadership is perhaps best illustrated through quotas established for soviet election campaigns. A rigorous attempt to gain increased participation by people of proletarian class origin had been outlined in the method of election for the First National Congress of Soviet Deputies in November 1931 ("Pengpeng bobo de Zhongguo suweiai yundong"). At the township level, every five workers and agricultural laborers were to elect one representative, while only one representative per fifty poor peasants, middle peasants and "others" was allowed. This proportion was to be maintained at every level. From each district, every twenty workers and agricultural laborers were to have one representative, while every two hundred poor peasants and middle peasants and people in the "other" category were to elect one representative. In the cities, every fifty workers were to elect one representative, and every five hundred people of other class backgrounds were entitled to a representative.

As Philip Huang points out in his study of Xingguo county, new election regulations formulated at the Congress for subsequent elections made no special provision for worker representation. However, insistence on the literal application of proletarian leadership persisted, so that by 1933, new election regulations had once again reinstated preferential selection for the proletariat. Clearly, Wang Ming's position on the question of proletarian leadership was not easily eliminated.

To sum up the quota issue, then, it was a question of using gong-gu-ku quotas as one further means to achieve proletarian leadership, vs. the position that broader mass participation through other kinds of quotas, or no quotas at all, should be achieved. In the view of those who supported the second position, since poor and middle peasants were the majority of oppressed people, and peasant women the most oppressed group of all, suffering both class oppression and male oppression, they, too, were potential activists in the anti-feudal revolution.

## The Land Investigation Movement and the Poor Peasant Corps

The Land Investigation Movement was formally launched on June 1, 1933, by the Council of People's Commissars of the Provisional Central Government of the Chinese Soviet Republic, headed by Mao Ze-dong ("Zhonghua suweiai gongheguo linshi...," 1933.6.1). The document stated that in many places within the Central Soviet Area, "the peasant masses have not yet been mobilized to the largest possible extent." Class struggle was to be intensified, with the proper class line being "to follow the leadership of the working class in the rural districts, to rely on the poor peasants, and to unite closely with the middle peasants so as to launch a determined assault on the feudal and semi-feudal forces" (Hsiao's translation, 1969: 198-199). Complete reinvestigation and redistribution of land was not the point of the movement. Rather, it was to uncover rich peasants and landlords who had in one way or another, concealed and retained land and property that should have been given over to workers, poor peasants, and middle peasants. The poor peasant corps was designated as "the most important mass organization" in the Land Investigation Movement, with small groups of agricultural laborers to be the "leading spirit of the corps."

The best study to date of the Land Investigation Movement is that of Trygve Lötveit in his work *Chinese Communism 1931-1934*. In Lötveit's words, "the rural class policy followed a zigzag course, but its general tendency was toward the left" (Lötveit, 1973: 145). He uses the development of increasingly harsh treatment of rich peasants and landlords, and the misclassificiation of many middle peasants as rich peasants during the course of the Land Investigation Movement, as examples of the trend toward the left. He attributes this development primarily to the increasing influence of the 28 Bolsheviks within the Central Soviet Area after the Central Committee moved there in late 1932 or early 1933. Specifically, Zhang Wen-tian, one of the 28 Bolsheviks also known as Luo Fu, took over from Mao the position of Chairman of the Council of People's Commissars in January 1934, and was responsible for changing the Land Investigation Movement from a broad mass movement to a leftist exercise in expressing revolutionary fervour. This resulted in excessive persecution of class enemies by many cadres at the local level (Lötveit, 1973: 145-184).

I agree with Lötveit that left errors in class policy were made during the 1934-phase of the Land Investigation Movement, but have tried to illustrate that this tendency was present throughout the entire period beginning in 1928. Therefore, I approach the Land Investigation Movement from the point of view of the previous over-emphasis on agricultural laborers. I interpret Mao's stress at the beginning of the movement on the poor peasant corps as a vehicle to mobilize as broad a mass base as possible, as an important move in opposition to Wang Ming and his supporters in the area of mass organizing.

In Mao's "Outline of the Organization and Work of the Poor Peasant Corps" of July 1933, he stated emphatically that the poor peasant corps was *not* an organization of only one class, but was rather an organization for the "vast poor peasant masses" of the soviet areas (Mao, 1933.7.15). This was a very different concept from the agricultural laborer union, an independent class organization for only the rural proletariat. Now, instead, the poor peasant corps was to join together as many people from the poor peasant, middle peasant and working classes as possible, to participate together in revolutionary activity. The vanguard function of agricultural laborers was still mentioned, but the main point was now to have them *within* the poor peasant corps. The persistence of the idea that agricultural laborers could become a proletarian vanguard reflected the fact that many policies during 1933-34 were not clear statements of any one particular point of view, but rather that the 28 Bolsheviks and Mao's forces often cooperated and combined their ideas on issues of major importance.

At the beginning of the Land Investigation Movement, the danger of alienating middle peasants by following too harsh a policy line toward rich peasants was also made clear. In a preliminary sum-up report written by Mao in August, he stated that some mistakes in classification had been made, and therefore middle peasants had said: "To be a middle peasant is dangerous. Just one step higher and I shall become a rich peasant." And so Mao concluded: "Any misconceptions about the rich peasants would doubtless also exert an adverse effect on the middle peasants (Mao, 1933.8; Hsiao's translation, 1969: 254). Thus, rich peasants were allowed a portion of poor land to work and middle peasants were not to give up any of their property for redistribution unless they consented. Careful attention to the interests not only of agricultural laborers and poor peasants, but also to those of middle peasants, was essential "to win over the majority of the masses" (Hsiao, 1969: 252).

The August report went on to say that in general, the Land Investigation Movement was going quite well. Many rich peasants and landlords had been successfully uncovered. But just as important, land investigation had become "a broad mass movement" and as a result, all revolutionary work had been increasing:

> In places where the land investigation has been successful, tremendous accomplishments have been made in expanding the Red Army and local armed forces, in selling economic construction bonds, in developing cooperatives, in the autumn harvesting and autumn plowing, in developing labor mutual-help societies, and in culture-building enterprises such as clubs, night schools, primary schools, and so on. All work has been going on more smoothly. On the basis of mass dynamism, large numbers of active elements have voluntarily and creatively become cadres in every kind of work. Many worker and peasant activists have joined the party and undertaken work in the soviets (Mao, 1933.8; Hsiao's translation with some alteration, 1969:237).

Thus, the most successful comrades were those who had properly understood "the close relationships between the land investigation drive and the revolutionary war." This was an important synthesis—a realization that if class struggle was carried out properly in terms of the land question, then every aspect of soviet life would benefit.

Bosheng county (formerly Ningdu—renamed in January 1933; see Hatano, 1961: 746) provides a brief case study of the role of the poor peasant corps in the positive work of land investigation in the Central Soviet Area. The Land Investigation Movement was designed primarily for those counties in which the initial stages of land reform were either carried out poorly or where they had not yet really begun in earnest. Bosheng was a county of the first type.

Citing the achievements of the Land Investigation Movement, Mao's August report praised Bosheng, along with Ruijin, as the two most successful counties (Mao, 1933.8). 406 recalcitrant landlords had been uncovered in Bosheng and 326 rich peasants, for a total of 20,000 mou of land that should have rightfully been redistributed among agricultural laborers and poor peasants (Jiangxi shengwei, 1933.9). Also, during the movement, it had been discovered that the former chairman of the Bosheng city soviet government, Peng Zi-zhong, had been making concessions to rich peasants and landlords. Before the struggle was launched against Peng, the city party committee had not paid much attention to the Land Investigation Movement. But many discussions among the masses had rectified this situation. Through criticism of Peng, the people became agitated and went out themselves to search for hidden property of landlords and rich peasants. As a result, it was decided in Bosheng to put both the land investigation committee and the confiscation and distribution committee of the soviet under direct control of the poor peasant corps (Jiangxi shengwei, 1933.9; Zhong Ping, 1933). Thus, the success of the Land Investigation Movement in Bosheng was directly attributable to its nature as a true mass movement. Through the poor peasant corps, for the first time, the people of Bosheng had actively undertaken the work of land confiscation and redistribution themselves.

As I have already indicated, the initial positive direction of the Land Investigation Movement was ultimately subverted due to the influence of Zhang Wen-tian. The major problem under his leadership of land investigation was the reoccurence of excessively harsh treatment of rich peasants—confiscation of all their land and other possessions. But the initial direction of the movement had set an important precedent for all future mass movements led by the party. It had as its goal to unite the majority of rural people, workers and peasants alike, around a common goal which they themselves worked to fulfill.

Thus, in the course of a mass movement around the issue of land investigation, Mao's goal was to have transformed the poor peasant corps into a mass organization serving the mutual interests of agricultural laborers, poor peasants, and middle peasants. Landlords and rich peasants who withheld surplus property were now forced to give it up through direct confrontation with members of the poor peasant corps. Organizing agricultural laborer unions had not generated mass involvement. On the other hand, the poor peasant corps, at least in some places in the Central Soviet Area, mobilized the majority of the rural population to act in the mutual interests of all oppressed rural people.

## Proletarian Leadership and the Chinese Revolution

The lessons learned by the party in its struggle to deal with the agricultural laborer question were of profound significance in developing a new application of proletarian leadership to the concrete realities of China. As Marxists, the Chinese communists were convinced of the theoretical formulation advanced by Marx—that since the development of capitalism "the proletariat alone is a really revolutionary class" (Marx and Engels, 1968: 44). In Marx's view, out of the development of the growing class antagonism between capital on the one hand, which takes away from wage laborers both the means of production and of subsistence, and the workers on the other, the conditions making possible a new mode of production—socialism—would arise. The exploitation experienced by the working class, the people who carried out the advanced form of socialized, cooperative labor under capitalism, would enable them to see the basic contradiction between the social organization of production, and private ownership of the means of production on the part of the capitalists. This would enable the workers, then, to raise a new demand for collective ownership and socially coordinated production as the only means that would expand the ability to produce still more efficiently. It was their role in the production process itself that would cause the workers to strive for the combination of socialized labor with collective ownership, eliminating the basis of capitalist exploitation through wage labor in the old form, as well as the possibility of exploitation in the future (Marx, 1967: 762-763).

What the Chinese communists had to confront in their practical application of these ideas about the proletariat to the Chinese situation was the fact that in China, capitalism did not exist to any great extent, either in the city or in the countryside. What could proletarian leadership mean to a group of communists who were striving, in the course of a revolution for peasant rights in the feudal countryside, for the ultimate goal of socialism? On the one hand, they could have taken the view that as long as they were confined to the Chinese countryside, nothing really revolutionary was possible. This is the implication of the interpretation presented by Harold Isaacs in his book, *The Tragedy of the Chinese Revolution.*

Written in 1938, the appendix to Isaacs' book entitled "The Rise and Fall of 'Soviet China' " deplores the fact that throughout the years 1927 to 1934, the party failed to re-ally itself with workers in Chinese cities and, therefore, in his estimation, failed to become a true party of the proletariat. After spending time in Moscow, reading many of the documents which are also considered here, Isaacs became aware of the effort, under Wang Ming's leadership, to rely on agricultural laborers as an alternative means to insure proletarian leadership of the Chinese revolution. Viewing the marginal role that agricultural laborers and other rural workers played in the rural Chinese economy as the primary reason this effort failed, Isaacs says:

> Working singly or in twos or threes, scattered on the land, in the villages, or itinerant, these workers occupied a subsidiary position in the peasant economy. The capitalist cannot exist without the factory worker, but the peasant can get along without a hired hand. In the sense that they were divorced from the means of production and sold their labor power for wages, these workers were proletarians. The fact that they were scattered and played no independent role in production meant, however, that they tended to form part of the general petty bourgeois mass of the peasantry. They could not, in any case, play an independent political role. It was impossible to base any consistent policy upon their interests (Isaacs, 1961: 345).

This insight into the working situation of agricultural laborers was substantially correct. However, on this basis, Isaacs concluded that since there were no legitimate workers in the soviet areas, it was completely impossible to organize for revolutionary activity in the Chinese countryside.

Fortunately for the history of the Chinese revolution, party members who followed Mao Ze-dong's leadership drew a very different conclusion. Mao, too, recognized the futility of attempting to independently organize and mobilize agricultural laborers, but realized instead that what should be done was to unite all oppressed people in the countryside to win the anti-feudal revolution. At the same time, the party itself, even during the bourgeois-democratic phase of the revolution, would take into account the historical, world-wide trend of the development of capitalism, and the *perspective* of the proletariat—namely, a thorough appreciation of what the benefits of socialized production and collective ownership could ultimately mean for all exploited people.[9] Thus, proletarian leadership for the Chinese revolution would be provided by a Communist Party which actively recruited members from among the rural population and worked for peasant demands for land reform and political power—goals which would, in and of themselves, move the struggle ahead, making socialist revolution throughout China a possibility for the future. Instead of class background, Mao stressed the importance of party members becoming "proletarianized in ideology" (Mao, 1945 "Resolutions. . .": 176, 212). This was quite different from Wang Ming's literal attempt to secure working class leaders for the revolution, mainly from among the agricultural laborers.

The reasons that neither independent organizations of agricultural laborers, nor attempts to insure their political leadership, succeeded in moving the Chinese revolution forward during this critical period may be summarized as follows: First, Comintern analysts and their followers supposedly acknowledged, as a result of their struggle against Li Li-san, that there would have to be two distinct stages through which the Chinese revolution would proceed, the first anti-feudal, the second anti-capitalist. But the struggle of agricultural laborers as proposed under Wang Ming's influence was designed primarily to fight against rich peasants, the representatives of capitalism in the Chinese countryside. Objectively, then, it negated the strategic importance of the two-stage revolution. As revolutionary practice would eventually show, the principal task of the first stage of the revolutionary process had to be the thorough uprooting of feudal landlordism because this was the major form of exploitation in rural China prior to 1949. Only after the successful completion and consolidation of land equalization in the early 1950s, could the effort to eliminate "rich peasant tendencies" among all peasants begin. This struggle against tendencies arising from the nature of small ownership within the rural economy—to accumulate private property and profit, and to perpetuate independent petty production—was subsequently begun during collectivization after 1952 and continues in China to the present day.

Secondly, even if rich peasants had not become the principal target of independent organizations of the rural proletariat, in terms of revolutionary tactics, this was an inappropriate organizational form for generating broad-based mass participation in the countryside. No one within the party leadership, from Mao Ze-dong to Wang Ming, denied that agricultural laborers could become active participants in the revolutionary process, based on the fact that as wage laborers they were among the most exploited people in rural society. But as long as the emphasis was placed on their independent role, their already-existing isolation from the rest of the rural population was perpetuated and their potential for combined efforts with poor peasants against feudal landlord-peasant relations never realized. Ultimately, these policies had developed through a rigid and mechanical application of the concept of proletarian leadership to China's rural revolution by urban intellectuals who, in the early 1930s, had not yet allied themselves with the peasant movement for land reform. Only through working first for widespread mass involvement in this stage of revolutionary struggle could the groundwork be laid for a socialist revolution in the future.

[1] The Chinese word for agricultural laborer is *gunong*—literally, "hired peasant."

[2] Chen Zheng-mo was the researcher responsible for this study of agricultural labor conditions throughout China in the 1930s. His research method was to send out a questionnaire of 15 questions to contacts supplied to him by other people working in agricultural research. He sent one questionnaire to each of 890 counties throughout China and received 726 questionnaires in response (Chen, 1935: 1). On this basis, he attempted to make generalizations for all of China and to say something about differences in working conditions, wages, terms of employment, the number of workers, and so on, from province to province. In 1955, Chen's data on the percentage of workers in each province and for all of China were reprinted in a compendium of statistical materials on China's modern economic history (Yen, et al., 1955: 263). The editors of the volume appended an editorial note to the table indicating that Chen's figures included both long and short-term workers and probably even a portion of the poor peasants. Therefore, they felt that the number of agricultural laborers was certainly less that Chen's estimate. The significance of the data, in their opinion, and the point I also want to make, is that the number of agricultural laborers in China was comparatively small, an indication that agricultural capitalism was not developed to any great extent.

[3] A second result of this analysis as it related to rural class struggle was the "hard-line" approach advocated toward rich peasants, the employers of agricultural laborers. Means to fight against rich peasants and favor agricultural laborers were included in land and tax laws promulgated within the soviet areas. Measures for taking an "anti-rich peasant line" in land reform were outlined in the "Land Law of the Chinese Soviet Republic" of 1931. All rich peasant land was to be confiscated initially, and they were to receive only poor land in return on the condition that they themselves would work it. Also, their surplus tools and farm buildings were to be confiscated (Diyici quanguo suweiai dahui, 1931.12.1). On the other hand, tax laws of the Soviet Republic stipulated that agricultural laborers who received land did not even have to pay land tax (Lötveit, 1973: 153).

[4] There is some confusion concerning identification of all 28 Bolsheviks, the exact dates of their travel to the soviet areas, and especially, the date of the move of the Central Committee to the Central Soviet Area. See Lötveit, pp. 10-11 and pp. 214-215, for a discussion of these problems. The most complete list of the 28 Bolsheviks was compiled by Sheng Yueh, a member of the group, and was published in 1971 (Sheng, 1971: 216). Sheng states that the majority of the 28 Bolsheviks returned to China in the summer of 1930 and settled in Shanghai (Sheng, 1971: 236). Sheng further dates the move of the Central Committee as "around November and December, 1932" (244), but the official party record of events dates this move in early 1933 (Mao, 1945 "Resolutions. . .": 185).

[5] I have been unable to determine who used this pen name. Perhaps it was a Hebei party member with strong ties to the 28 Bolshevik faction who wrote for *Red Flag* at this time. It does not seem to have been used by any of the 28 Bolsheviks themselves.

[6] Case histories relating the conditions of both long and short-term agricultural laborers are found throughout the Xingguo report. See especially the section on gunong, beginning on p. 222.

[7] Unfortunately, there are no better population statistics available. Since this paper considers

policies implemented primarily in the Central Soviet Area in southern Jiangxi and western Fujian, a more precise estimate for only that area would be desirable. However, since most of the soviets were situated in relatively poor, isolated areas, like southern Jiangxi and western Fujian, the estimate of 3% of the population of *all* the soviet areas as workers would probably have been accurate for the Central Soviet Area as well.

[8] The 24% figure may actually seem high, but was probably close to the limit of rural workers that could have joined the army. Most agricultural laborers in the areas first occupied by the Red Army had already been urged to join the army in the early years of the revolution (Grigor'ev, 1975: 31-32).

[9] Furthermore, Marx had also pointed out that even under conditions in which a significant proletariat exists in numbers, workers acting in isolation from an organized communist party representing their interests, would not have the capacity to systematically plan for action which would lead to socialism. For aside from the working class capacity to appreciate cooperative labor, there is also the strong tendency for workers to view each other as enemies, based on the competitive conditions under which they must seek work in the first place (Marx and Engels, 1968: 43).

# The Party and Peasant Women*
## Kathy Le Mons Walker

From 1931 to 1934, the Chinese Communist Party successfully developed a revolutionary movement among peasant women. Through this movement, a majority of women who lived within rural base areas under party leadership participated in revolutionary struggle. In this process, they raised their status and expanded their roles and activities. This paper will consider the party's policy of integrating the struggle for the liberation of peasant women into the total revolutionary effort in the soviet areas, and the methods developed to secure mass participation of women in social revolution.

**Setting the Direction: 1931**

1931 was a critical year in the development of the revolutionary movement in the soviet areas. Four years earlier, in 1927, a party leadership comprised mainly of urban intellectuals had been forced to shift its emphasis from urban areas to the countryside. Largely under the direction of Mao Ze-dong and Zhu De, the party then began to devise a strategy for agrarian revolution which would bridge the gap between its urban orientation and the realities of the Chinese countryside. Between 1928 and 1930, eleven main revolutionary bases were established. Initial land distribution in those areas created the basis for support from the peasants. Yet the party was far from having established a solid bond with the rural population. The new bases were not stable, solidified areas. The primary task during those years was to militarily consolidate the areas

---

*Author's note: My thanks to Norma Diamond, Linda Grove, and Dennis Engbarth for their comments on an earlier draft of this article. I would especially like to thank Professor Lucie Hirata, whose help in a special Documents Reading Course enabled me to "get off the ground" when I first began translating the handwritten Jiangxi materials, and Jane Wheeler, for the use of several Jiangxi documents which she translated in the reading course.

and begin the process of establishing political institutions. The military situation necessitated the hasty absorption of new cadres to take over the political work, often without training. Because of the organizational weakness of the party as a whole, and the "opportunism" of many of the new cadres who were often rich peasants (Isaacs, 1961: 343-44) or lumpenproletarians (see Philip Huang's article in this volume), party policies and directives were frequently ignored at lower levels (Kim, 1973: 40). Local leadership was not drawn to any significant degree from among the poor peasants in early organizing efforts. As a result, in many areas the attitude of peasants towards new political forms was, as one party leader reported, "passive and acquiescent at best" (Kim, 1973: 45).

Thus, in 1931, a primary concern was the need to politically consolidate the areas which were already under Red Army control. In practice, this meant developing the organization and methods to go "deep into the villages" and to activate the peasants to participate in revolutionary struggle. Despite factional differences and tensions, and the continuing emphasis on urban revolution among a portion of party leadership, there was consensus on the primary tasks within the soviet areas (Mao, 1945 "Resolutions. . .": 192, 210).

In 1931, the party began the implementation of a series of reorganization and reconstruction programs. These programs were intended chiefly to develop a sounder political structure, to replace old ineffective leadership with newly recruited activist cadres, and to develop a mass revolutionary movement among the peasants (Kim, 1973: 38-39). In the following years there was a continued application of new social and economic programs aimed at furthering the anti-feudal revolution while deepening and widening mass participation in revolutionary activity. Among these programs were new policies for the peasant women's movement which reflected the evolution of party thinking on the role of the movement and on the concrete methods for developing it.

Since the early 1920s the emancipation of women had been proclaimed as one of the party's revolutionary goals. The party had pursued a basic policy of uniting the struggle for women's liberation with the revolutionary movement. As the soviet areas were established, a women's program was formulated which called for the legal equality of men and women, freedom of marriage and divorce, opposition to oppression of women in the family, and the full entry of women into economic, political and cultural life. In 1931, as part of the larger process of evaluation and reorganization, the party conducted an extensive assessment of the women's movement in the soviet areas. This assessment revealed that the movement had made little progress (Zhonggong suqu zhongyangju, 1931.2.26).

From the 1931 perspective, the lack of progress was attributable to the general failure to activate the rural populace as well as to problems unique to the women's movement. The most serious of these special problems was the reluctance of intermediate and lower-level leadership to accept or promote the peasant women's movement. Male chauvinism, the intensity of women's oppression in the countryside, and the lack of cadre training led many male cadres to ignore party directives on the development of the movement. Few cadres had been recruited from among peasant women. In many areas there was no planned, systematic, or regular work among women (Zhonggong zhongyang weiyuanhui, 1930.4.5; Xiang-E-Gan sheng weiyuanhui, 1932.1.14; Wu Mei, 1930b).

Although not as widespread as the male leadership's "right error of liquidating the women's movement," "left errors" of young female cadres, most of whom were of urban educated background, also inhibited the development of the movement. Lack of training and a tendency to approach the movement from the perspective of those aspects crucial to their own liberation, caused these cadres to stress the priority of women's issues over that of social revolution (Zhonggong zhongyang Ganbei tebie weiyuanhui, 1931.3.3). Freedom of marriage became the focus of their work. In the party's view to focus solely on women's issues was destructive to revolutionary unity, for it obscured the class basis of women's oppression and the relationship of that oppression to the revolutionary struggle. It caused the women's movement to become isolated, neither lending strength to, nor receiving support from, the general struggle (Shaogong beilu zhiwei qingfu shuji lianxi weiyuanhui, 1931.3; Ba Zhen, 1932; Zhonggong suqu zhongyangju, 1931.2.26).

Party and women's movement leaders also recognized characteristics of the condition of peasant women which inhibited their active participation. The most important of these was that the long period of bondage and oppression of peasant women had caused them to internalize the sexist thinking of society and to take it as their own standard for thought and action. As a result, peasant women were hesitant to believe that they had the power to revolt (Sifa xingzhengbu diaochaju, 1961: 36-37).

In a call to analyze past mistakes and establish a new direction in woman-work, the party's Central Bureau of the Soviet Areas explained that the basic line for the women's movement henceforth was to lead peasant women to "participate in all of the revolutionary struggles and in the midst of struggle train them to do revolutionary work" (Zhonggong suqu zhongyangju, 1931.2.26). The Central Bureau stressed that while women from lower levels were to be trained as supervisory personnel for the women's movement, at the same time they were to be trained to direct other kinds of revolutionary work, "thereby opposing the idea that the women's movement is restricted to questions of women themselves" (Zhonggong suqu zhongyangju, 1931.2.26).

Party leaders had become increasingly aware of the necessity of politically activating peasant women in order to realize overall revolutionary goals. The new policy demonstrated that as party thinking evolved on the means of successfully waging agrarian revolution and revolutionary war, there was a new recognition of the crucial role of the peasant women's movement in the process. In contrast with the earlier conception of peasant women as merely a support force for the revolutionary war (Zhonggong zhongyang weiyuanhui, 1930.4.5), peasant women were now to be trained as "leaders of the masses" in order to "make them the mainstay of the consolidation work and of the expansion of the soviet movement" (Zhonggong zhongyang Ganbei tebie weiyuanhui, 1931.3.3; *Hongse Zhonghua,* 1932.3.6).

The new direction in the women's movement was an essential part of the party's general effort to integrate itself with the rural populace. It paralleled the work of politically activating workers and peasants in the soviet areas by gaining their participation in government and in new social and economic programs. As will be discussed below, such an approach enabled the party simultaneously to carry through social revolution and mobilize the population for war. This approach did not lessen emphasis on the struggle for women's liberation. On the contrary, involving peasant women as participants and leaders in all areas of revolutionary struggle implied a radical break with their traditional roles. It was a positive means of combatting the oppression of women in the countryside while minimizing male-female conflicts. At the same time, struggle for the implementation of the women's program remained a focus and widened the scope of agrarian revolution. But as in the general revolutionary movement, the central task of the women's movement was the consolidation and expansion of the soviets and mobilization for war. For in the party's view, without the victory of the primary struggle, genuine liberation for women and men would be impossible (Ba Zhen, 1932).[1]

The policy formulations of 1931 set the course for the development of the peasant women's movement in the soviet areas. They were consistently supported by Mao Ze-dong, who by holding the two top posts in the government until 1934, was in a position to greatly influence their implementation. At the same time, female members of the "28 Bolsheviks" filled some of the major leadership positions in the women's movement.[2] Their assumption of these positions probably lent strength to the new orientation of the movement toward integration with the total revolutionary effort. Mao's later positive assessment of mass work in the soviet areas (Mao, 1945 "Resolutions. . .": 210) suggests that despite other differences between Mao and the Returned Students, their efforts were mutually reinforcing in the areas of woman-work as one crucial aspect of generating mass participation in the rural areas. On a less speculative level, it is clear that from 1931 to 1934, three factors worked to produce significant results in the women's movement: first, increased party support insured that the basic policies and programs for women were implemented; second, the development of new methods and organizational forms activated women politically; and third, war mobilization put intensified pressure on intermediate and lower-level leadership to accept and encourage the participation of women in the party, in politics, and production, for as the needs of war expanded in many areas the maintenance of production and soviet political power at the local level became in large part, the responsibility of women (Mao, 1933.12.15: 165; see Philip Huang's article in this volume on the relation between war mobilization and women in the specific case of Xingguo county).

**Strengthening Party Leadership**

At the heart of the new 1931 policies regarding women was the need to strengthen party leadership of the peasant women's movement. As a first step, the party called for the immediate establishment of Women's Committees within those party and Youth League organizations which had previously failed to do so. The Women's Committees were to be responsible for woman-work at each level of party organization, culminating in the Women's Committee of the Central Committee (Zhonggong zhongyang Ganbei tebie weiyuanhui, 1931.3.3). As party and government reorganization proceeded in 1931-32, a period in which the establishment and strengthening of local party organizations was a major goal, the party stressed the need to develop women's movement personnel at the township (*xiang*) level (Ningdu linshi xian weiyuanhui, 1932.4.21).

The recruitment of female party members was another basic concern. As part of the developing theories of mass-line leadership, recruitments were to be made primarily from those women who emerged as activists and who had the respect of local women. These women were viewed as having the most potential for fulfilling the functions of good cadres—namely, the ability to create the concrete methods for mobilizing and integrating themselves with the people (Mao, 1933.12.15: 125-126). To reach more deeply into the countryside, thus avoiding the type of errors made earlier, the party aimed to create a core of activist female cadres who supported and understood the problems of local people.

To encourage recruitment, the Jiangxi Provincial Party Committee in mid-1932 set a goal of 15% female membership (Jiangxi shengwei, 1932.6.12). County party committees also established targets for local recruitment (Ningdu linshi xianwei, 1932.4.21). By early 1933, female party membership in Jiangxi Province had reached 11% of total membership (Jiangxi shengwei, 1933.9.20).

In a major recruitment drive launched by the Jiangxi party in conjunction with the Land Investigation Movement and soviet election campaign in mid-1933, female recruitment, along with that of "workers" was strongly emphasized ("workers" included industrial workers and handicraft apprentices, agricultural laborers, and coolies; see Lynda Bell's article in this volume for a discussion of this term). The goal was to double the number of women party members. The three-month drive was highly successful, with 29,548 new members added to the party. At the conclusion of the drive, women comprised 20% of the 97,451 members in the Jiangxi party (Jiangxi shengwei, 1933.9.20).

In 1932, efforts were again intensified to increase women members. The party launched a campaign for each party member to recruit one new female member so that "not a single, active, progressive laboring woman" would be left outside the party ("Xuexi Xingguo Fantai qu fazhan nü dangyuan mofan"). By constantly re-emphasizing the importance of recruitment among women, significant gains in female membership were made throughout 1933-34.

Cadre training was yet another area of general concern for both men and women. Lack of training was cited as a principal cause of the commandist and bureaucratic workstyles so prevalent among cadres (Kim, 1973: 191-92). In the women's movement these problems were acute. In the pre-1931 period, women often had been chosen simply to fill positions. Lacking training, they executed their work in an authoritarian or perfunctory manner, and thus failed to win the support of local women (Zhonggong suqu zhongyangju, 1931.2.26). Therefore, along with the recruitment of female party members, the 1931 directives stressed the development of female cadre training programs (Zhonggong zhongyang Ganbei tebie weiyuanhui, 1931.3.3). Furthermore, education about the women's movement was not confined to women's movement cadres, but was included in new training programs for all cadres. For example, a short-term training class organized for cadres in 1932 included "The

Building of the Soviets and the Women's Movement" as a major lecture topic (Ningdu zhongxin xianwei, 1932.4.5).

Party leadership of the women's movement was also strengthened by the implementation of the new policy of "collective leadership." This system was designed to eliminate the extreme authoritarian control exercised by many party secretaries in the pre-1931 period and to implement the party's organizational line of "maintaining contact with the masses both inside and outside the party" (Mao, 1945 "Resolutions. . .": 205). Under this system, the chairs of various functional committees at each level of organization were grouped together into an executive committee for collective decision-making (Deng, 1932). By 1933, collective leadership had been implemented effectively in many party organizations (Jiangxi shengwei, 1933.9.20). Thus, under this system the chairperson of the Women's Committee had the opportunity to participate in all planning and decision-making sessions of the executive committee, and to promote support from that committee for the women's movement.

These attempts to strengthen woman-work within the party reflect the new level of support given the women's movement after 1931. They indicate that the party aimed to realize in practice the stated belief that "woman-work is part of our whole revolutionary work and it must be integrated into the work of our revolution" (Zhonggong zhongyang Ganbei tebie weiyuanhui, 1931.3.3). Successes within the party were matched by parallel efforts in mass work in the villages to implement women's policies.

### New Organizational Forms

By 1931, party leadership understood clearly that if the basic policies of the women's movement were to be implemented, an effective organizational structure for women, both within and outside the party, must be provided. In the pre-1931 period, party guidelines had called for, in addition to party organizations, two types of women's organizations: Woman-Work Committees, units of the soviet governments which were responsible for transmitting women's policies and work plans to mass organizations (Zhonggong suqu zhongyangju, 1931.2.26); and Women's Sections of Poor Peasant Corps, conceived as the basic organizations for organizing and mobilizing peasant women (Zhonggong zhongyang weiyuanhui, 1929.12.1). But like the party organization itself, these organizations had not been widely established or had functioned poorly at the local level. Woman-Work Committees were often constituted in name only, and in many areas Poor Peasant Corps failed to become functioning organizations (Kim, 1973: 16-17, 127; Roy, 1946: 631). In conjunction with efforts in other areas to secure mass participation at the local level, such as the construction of local soviets, and in order to combat some of the special problems of the women's movement, the party in 1931 abolished Woman-Work Committees and created two new organizational forms for women (Zhonggong suqu zhongyangju, 1931.2.26).

The more important of the new organizations were the Congresses of Women Workers and Peasant Women, at first called Congresses of Laboring Women in some areas. Through them the party attempted to create a more appropriate medium for providing leadership of the women's movement, promoting new leaders from among the local women, and obtaining the participation of large numbers of women in revolutionary activity (Zhonggong suqu zhongyangju, 1932.2.20).

Often in the soviet areas a new campaign or concept was tested first in one or two areas as a "pilot program" after which it was initiated on a wider scale. Such was the case with the Congresses. After being successfully developed in Ruijin, they were established in other areas (Ba Zhen, 1932). Initially, due to variations in local party organizations, the introduction of the congresses was sporadic, but by 1933 they were functioning throughout the soviet areas (Mao, 1934.1.24/25).

When the congresses were first established some cadres voiced criticism of them. In particular, they felt that the danger existed of these organizations "being in opposition to soviet political power" (Zhonggong suqu zhongyangju, 1932.2.20). These criticisms probably arose from continuing opposition to the women's movement among local male leadership, or from the fear that the congresses would become autonomous organizations concerned only with women's issues.

To clarify the "separate but integrated" nature of the congresses the Central Bureau of the Soviet Areas in early 1932 drafted an outline of their organization and work. It was emphasized that although the congresses were separate women's organizations, they were not autonomous groups meeting regularly. Rather, they were to be convened temporarily (usually every two to four weeks depending on need) by either the party, the district ($qu$) Committee for the Improvement of Women's Living Conditions, or the township soviet government. The congresses, stressed the Bureau, were party leadership organizations designed to form a link between the peasant women and the party. At each meeting of the local congress, a women's movement cadre from the local party branch was to attend, who "should, in fact, be the director of the women's representatives and should be officially approved by the congress" (Zhonggong suqu zhongyangju, 1932.2.20).

Normally a women's movement cadre from the party branch had responsibility for establishing the congress in an area. Using the village as a unit, the women of a village (landlord and rich peasant women excluded) were summoned to a mass meeting to elect representatives. Usually, 10 to 20 persons elected one representative. All the representatives from the villages of a township constituted the township congress. Each village also elected one chair, and the chairs of the villages, plus the local women's movement cadre, constituted the presidium of the township congress (Mao, 1933.12.15: 163; Ningdu zhongxin xianwei, 1932.7.17). Re-elections were held evey three to six months.

Once a congress was formed, its representatives, when possible, were to be notified of meetings and questions to be discussed in advance, to enable them to obtain the views of the local women before the meeting. Afterwards, representatives were to inform local women of the discussions and decisions of the meeting, either by reporting to the women in their vicinity individually, or through a mass meeting of the village women. In this way, through their local representatives, village women could be mobilized to carry out the concrete work of the women's movement (Zhonggong suqu zhongyangju, 1932.2.20).

The introduction of the congresses was an important step toward increasing the participation of women in revolutionary activity. Through them, the party was able to establish a direct link with village women. Separating the congresses from other organizations which were dominated by male leadership created the opportunity for women to gain political experience. The frequent re-elections and removal of ineffective representatives helped to minimize commandist and bureaucratic workstyles among the representatives, and to maximize the opportunity for large numbers of village women to gain leadership experience. The opportunity for the assumption of responsibility and participation in the congresses must have been a strong impetus for raising the revolutionary activism of many women, as well as raising their confidence and willingness to demand a share in political power.

The congresses also possessed the same organizational characteristics of the village and township soviet congresses which were so highly praised by Mao—a close relationship between a delegate and a group of individuals through the election of evenly distributed representatives who lived and worked among the people. Thus, the form was an important means of maximizing two-way communication between upper levels of organization and village women, and of preventing alienation of leaders from the people (Mao, 1934.1.24/25: 463). Like the soviets, the congresses were also undoubtedly a source of recruitment for women party members.

The second new organization created in 1931 was the Committee for the Improvement of Women's Living Conditions. Serving as intermediate organizations between the congresses and soviet governments, the committees were first established as special agencies of the soviet governments beginning at the district level. Presumably staffed by women's movement cadres with some training or experience, these committees worked closely with the women's congresses and party organizations, providing planning, direction, and leadership.

One of the primary functions of these committees at the district level was to investigate the concrete living conditions of the women in that district (Zhonggong zhongyang Ganbei tebie weiyuanhui, 1931.3.3). Statistical data on the conditions of women in a locality were compiled by the village representatives and then submitted to the committee. These investigations were a means of combatting the lack of knowledge and concern for the village women which had earlier plagued party and government organizations. On the basis of the investigations, plans for the concrete work of mobilizing the women's struggle could be formulated and presented to the women's congresses for discussion and implementation.

Another important function of the committees was to determine the effectiveness of lower-level governments in executing policy and regulations concerning women. Government neglect of or opposition to women's rights was a major problem. Mao cited this neglect as a deterrent to the political activation of women for the central task of war mobilization, and called on the soviet governments to give full attention to women's rights and to the enforcement of the marriage regulations (Mao, 1932.9.20: 132). To provide a check on this negligence or opposition the committeees were authorized to evaluate the work of the lower-level governments, report their findings to higher levels, and make recommendations to the women's congresses of action to be taken against backward local officials. To promote coordination between the work of the committees and the district governments, some county governments specified that the chair or members of the district committee should participate in each meeting of the presidium of the district government (Ganxian suweiai zhengfu, 1932.10.20).

The first joint meeting of the district Committee for the Improvement of Women's Living Conditins of Gonglue county, held in mid-1931, provides a good example of the leadership function of the committees. At the time of the meeting, the committee had been established in all districts of the county and initial investigations had been conducted. The principal topics of discussion at this meeting were the need for more thorough surveys, the creation of propaganda work to oppose oppression of women in the family, implementation of the marriage regulations, mobilization of women for participation in the revolutionary war, and questions of raising the level of women's culture and education. A number of concrete proposals and suggestions were made for mobilizing the women's struggle, such as a county-wide campaign against the beating of women by family members. Decisions made at this conference were to be reported to the district committees for discussion and then to the congresses, where the committees were to give direction and education to the representatives. Committee members were to conduct detailed discussions of the proposals and plans of action in order to give the representatives the level of knowledge and awareness necessary to mobilize the local women (Gonglue xian, 1931.7.8). The committees, then, provided leadership and direction for the peasant women's movement at the local level, and also helped to develop that movement on a systematic basis throughout each county.

The policies begun in 1931 were decisive factors in the successful building of the women's movement in the soviet areas. A corps of activist cadres, both inside and outside the party, was created to give systematic direction to the movement and to implement party policy locally. With the creation of the congresses a structure was provided through which cadres could effectively carry out work among local women. At the same time, village women were given the opportunity to gain political experience and to enter into revolutionary life. By 1933, in those areas where there was strong party leadership and an effective functioning of women's congresses, the women's movement was most successful in gaining female participation in all aspects of revolutionary activity (Mao, 1933: 183).

**Election Campaigns**

One of the new programs implemented during the reconstruction of the soviets in 1931 was the launching of mass election campaigns. As Philip Huang's article on Xingguo shows, these campaigns were expected to expand participation in the political processes, replace undesirable leadership with new activist cadres, and add to the development of a mass political movement—necessary components to the successful functioning of the soviet system of government. For the women's movement, the campaigns were, in addition, an important means of increasing the participation of women in the soviet governments and women's organizations, and recruiting new female cadres from among the activists who emerged during the election movement (Zhonggong zhongyang Ganbei tebie weiyuanhui, 1931.3.3; Jiangxi shengwei, 1933.10.11).

The first election campaign was begun in 1931 to elect representatives to the First National Congress, held near Ruijin in November 1931. Propaganda for the campaign called for special attention to be paid to recruiting women delegates. Election regulations issued in early 1931 by the Central Bureau specified that there should be at least twelve women among the 249 delegates from the soviet areas, selected according to geographical areas (Zhonggong zhongyang Ganbei tebie weiyuanhui, 1931.3.3). Although the number of women was only a small percentage of the delegates, given the limited work among women prior to 1931, it may have represented to the party a realistic percentage for recruitment. In the 1933 national election campaigns the quota was raised considerably.

As the election movement began, meetings were held in women's organizations, or mass meetings of village women were called. The meetings were designed to explain the meaning of the reconstruction and election campaign, and to discuss shortcomings of existing leadership and the selection of suitable delegates to the Congress. The meetings were also designed to actively involve large numbers of women in the women's movement by waging a propaganda campaign to raise the party's central slogans and women's program, and link them to the reconstruction of the soviets and consolidation of revolutionary power.

As an additional impetus to the women's movement, township women's committees were required to prepare "Women's Resolutions" to be discussed and adopted by the National Congress. As an outgrowth of discussions in the election meetings of village women, these resolutions gave the party and National Congress an indication of the opinions and problems of a large portion of the peasant women, and at the same time heightened the sense of involvement and influence in determining women's policy among the peasant women themselves (Zhonggong zhongyang Ganbei tebie weiyuanhui, 1931.3.3).

Subsequent elections for new local congresses were held in early 1932 ("Zhonghua suweiai gongheguo de xuanju xize"). They were not as intensive as those for the First National Congress. Their primary purpose, as Philip Huang's Xingguo article indicates, was to continue the reconstruction by expanding the recruitment of activists and eliminating those people who had failed to display leadership qualities. As such, they represented a further development toward the goal of attaining mass-line leadership. Depending on the quality of leadership in a locality, additional elections were held in some areas later in 1932 (Mao, 1933.12.15: 132).

Despite variation in different areas, the election campaigns of 1931-32 appear to have been successful in increasing the numbers of peasant women involved in both the women's movement and political participation in general. The simultaneous occurrence of the election campaigns with the establishment of women's congresses in many localities helped to activate those organizations as well. The two developments were, in fact, mutually reinforcing in forwarding the development of the peasant women's movement.

As for specific data on women and the election campaigns, female representatives comprised about 25% of the Changgang township congress in Xingguo county in 1932. In Caixi, in southwest Fujian, designated by Mao as a model township in the election movement, prior to the fall election in 1932, 30% of the representatives were women; after the fall elections the number of women increased to 60%, and climbed even higher in 1933 (Mao, 1933: 178-179).

Increased army recruitment among the male population was undoubtedly a significant factor in the rapid increase of female political representation in Caixi in 1932. However, in many other localities, massive recruitment for the army did not begin until 1933, according to census figures for a number of counties in the central soviet area ("Jiangxi shengsu baogao"). The major stimulus for the rising numbers of women representatives in the local congresses in 1931-32 appears to have been the combination of the election campaigns, new organizational forms, and other mass mobilization policies for drawing women into the women's movement, rather than solely the effects of large-scale male recruitment for the army.

In the fall of 1933 another massive election campaign was conducted for selection of delegates to the Second National Congress and for the reconstitution of local soviets. It coincided with other political campaigns—the Land Investigation Movement which began in the summer of 1933, a drive for army recruitment, and a campaign to elect delegates for a Provincial Congress of Women Workers and Peasant Women.

The campaign and preparatory work for the Provincial Congress of Women Workers and Peasant Women, held in December 1933, was expected to strengthen the women's movement, to mobilize peasant women to join in the soviet elections, and, in conjunction with other political campaigns, to generate new levels of activism in the revolutionary movement, especially for the central task of war mobilization (Jiangxi shengwei, 1933.10.11). In the face of increased war mobilization party guidelines for the women's and National Congress elections stressed the urgent need to develop and train women cadres to take over political work. A quota of "at least 25%" female representation was set for the National Congress (Jiangxi shengwei, 1933.10.11).

Preparations for the women's congress extended over several months. After an initial joint conference of the heads of the county Women's Departments (the name was changed from Women's Committees to Women's Departments in 1933) and the official announcement of the congress by the Jiangxi Provincial Party Committee, joint conferences of the district Women's Departments in each county were held to formulate concrete plans for mobilization work. Following these conferences, meetings of local congresses and mass meetings of village women were called.

During the course of the campaign to elect women's congress representatives, existing leadership was called into question and faulty leaders replaced. In Guangchang county, for example, party leadership had been weak, the congresses in some townships were not functioning, attendance at congress meetings had been poor, and struggle for implementation of the marriage regulations had been minimal. At a preparatory meeting for the campaign, attended by the heads of the district Women's Departments in the county, these problems were discussed. Because of the low levels of achievement in the past, special education and propaganda methods were devised, such as locally organized propaganda teams who were to visit each woman in an area to publicize and discuss the campaign. Under the slogan of "not letting a single woman misunderstand the meaning of the provincial congress," the intensive efforts for the campaign were expected to double the number of women actively participating in women's organizations and organized for war support work (Guangchang zhongxin xianwei, 1933.11.2).

The combined campaigns in 1933 expanded the development of a mass political movement among women begun with the 1931-32 campaigns. Exceptionally large turn-outs for the soviet elections occurred. In many areas at least 80% of the population attended the election meetings (Mao, 1934.1.24/25: 259). The election meetings, which generated a spirit of mass enthusiasm, often resulted in large numbers of army volunteers and in the formation of new women's support groups for the army (such as laundress and sewing teams, *weilaodui* [cheer and entertainment corps], and transportation, first-aid, communications, and stretcher bearer corps) (Mao, 1933: 180; Jiangxi sheng funü lianhe hui (ed.), 1962: 2-3). Furthermore, the assumption of local leadership positions by women increased dramatically. After the elections many of the local soviet congresses contained at least 25% women representatives (Mao, 1934.1.24/25: 259).

In December, 1933, the Jiangxi Provincial Congress of Women Workers and Peasant Women also served the important function of raising the level of activism and increasing the sense of solidarity and unity among women. Delegates from different areas were able to become acquainted with one another and to discuss the work of the women's movement. Carrying their own quilts, chopsticks, and bowls, they first assembled in each county at the government headquarters and then proceeded to Ruijin, site of the provincial government offices. At the congress, the summing up of experiences, achievements, and problems in woman-work, as well as the formulation of new policies led to an increase in awareness and understanding of the movement among the delegates. After the congress, delegates were able to transmit their new committment to the work to congress representatives and village women (Geming funü de mofan").

The activism of women cadres following the congress was considered a major factor in the expansion of woman-work in the early months of 1934. Cadres conducted extensive political mobilization among local women, organizing task forces and propaganda teams to carry out house-to-house propaganda. Drawing on the increased enthusiasm which had been generated in the election campaigns, these intensive efforts produced spectacular results for the war effort. Quotas set at the congress for "provincial revolutionary competitions" were frequently surpassed. In one county, for example, 551 men were encouraged through female effort to join the Red Army, a figure which exceeded by 351 the competition goal of 200 new members; instead of 5,000 piars of straw shoes, the women of the county made 6,120 pairs; in the saving campaign, 425 *yuan* was collected rather than the projected 250 yuan; "strike forces" for the collection of grains were organized; and in the face of enemy attack, special women's teams for transportation, building of defense and other facilities were organized ("Geming funü de mofan").

## Improving the Quality of Peasant Women's Lives

Under the basic line of gaining women's participation in all of the revolutionary struggles, another important aspect of party policy after 1931 was to mobilize peasant women to "struggle against feudal oppression" and to participate in programs designed to improve the quality of peasant life. Mobilizing women for these purposes was part of the general party policy of emphasizing socio-economic programs to stimulate moblization for war (Mao, 1933.8.20: 129).

Underlying the general policy was the linking of politics and war, as well as the belief that a primary aspect of war mobilization was to simultaneously improve the economic well-being and living conditions of the people. Success in this area was contingent upon the development of leadership methods and programs which would convince people that the party represented their interests, and also the involvement of as many people as possible in the implementation of these programs (Mao, 1934.1.27; see also Mao, 1933.8.20; and Kim, 1973: 98-103). Summarizing this position at the Second National Congress Mao called on cadres to give their full attention to the "question of the immediate interests, the well-being of the broad masses. For the revolutionary war is a war of the masses; it can be waged only by mobilizing the masses and relying on them." He emphasized that it was necessary to do much more than simply mobilize the people to carry on the war. They should be led in the struggle for land distribution, their labor enthusiasm and agricultural production should be increased, and solutions should be found to the problems facing them—problems of food, shelter and clothing, sickness and hygiene, and marriage. "In short," he stated, "all the practical problems facing the masses' everyday life should claim our attention. If we attend to these problems, solve them and satisfy the needs of the masses, we shall really become organizers of the well-being of the masses and they will truly rally round us and give their warm support" (Mao, 1934.1.27: 147-148).

In this context, the party considered women's struggles against their subordinate position in the old feudal hierarchy an excellent vehicle of mobilization for social revolution. As such, these struggles were viewed as one means of raising the class consciousness of all peasants. The party emphasized that work in this area had to be accompanied by broad and deep propaganda to enable all of the people to thoroughly understand that "the struggle was in no way a 'men and women's struggle' in which women rise up to oppose men" (Ganxian suweiai zhengfu, 1932.10.20). The struggle was, rather, directed at the feudal system. Focussing the struggle on the class basis of women's oppression lent strength to and expanded the scope of the agrarian revolution, and created the possibility of support from both women and men.

As with other programs of the period, the party sought to raise the confidence, ability and revolutionary consciousness of local women through broad participation and collective struggle. The party, Committees for the Improvement of Women's Living Conditions, and women's congresses gave coordinated leadership and guidance to this work. Local women could report instances of familial oppression or government negligence in implementing policy to their representatives, who would in turn meet to discuss plans for mobilizing women in the area to take up the case (Zhonggong suqu zhongyangju, 1932.9.20). Through the congresses, area-wide campaigns were initiated, such as those to implement the marriage regulations, oppose the beating of women, and attack the practice of arranged marriage (Gonglue xian, 1931.7.8).

Women's congresses were also authorized to send representatives to the government to make formal charges against negligent government officials and to bring them or those who openly opposed women's policy to a congress or mass meeting of local women to account for their actions. Representatives could, in addition, go to higher levels of government to demand that cases of opposition be re-examined (Ningdu zhongxin xianwei, 1932.7.17; Zhonggong suqu zhongyangju, 1932.2.20). Thus, along with the Committees for the Improvement of Women's Living Conditions, the congresses provided a check on the government implementation of women's policy and were an important source for exerting pressure on unsupportive government personnel to change their policies.

Ningdu county, liberated in the fall of 1931, provides an example of how the movement worked. During the first six months after liberation little work among women was accomplished; with a population of 150,000 "laboring women" and a party membership of 1,700 for the county, only 20 female party members had been recruited. By April 1932, this "liquidationist error" was candidly recognized by the county party committee. A detailed work plan for the county's women's movement was issued, which set the basic responsibility for the party to lead the movement "to participate in the land revolution, to develop the revolutionary war, to break the bonds of the feudal system, and through the victory of the land revolution and anti-imperialist struggle to win the liberation of women" (Ningdu linshi xian weiyuanhui, 1932.4.21). Instructions were given for the establishment of women's congresses, and for conducting investigations of the class background and situation of the women in the county.

By July considerable progress had been made. Women's committees and congresses had been established and the principal demands of the women in the county had been determined (examples of such demands were: "oppose confiscating the land, grains, or property of a woman after divorce"; "oppose not letting women study and learn to read"; "oppose husbands who refuse to continue support of their former wives after a divorce or who refuse to let women work in the fields") (Ningdu zhongxin xianwei, 1932.7.14). At this time the county committee issued a directive, "The Program and Method for Mobilizing the Laboring Women's Struggle," which enumerated the various means women might utlize in satisfying their demands. The central theme of the directive was the importance of mobilizing women to struggle around specific issues rather than to simply rely on government orders, for it was in this way that the activism and political consciousness of the local women would be raised.

Shortly after this directive was issued, two cases involving women's oppression were brought to the attention of the county committee. First, a male peasant, apparently as a result of a disagreement, sliced his wife's neck with a sickle, cut off her ears, and then killed her. The second case involved a security officer in one of the village governments, who every few days with little apparent provocation came home and beat his wife. Unable to stand this treatment any longer, the woman went to the local government for assistance. The county committee decided to use these two cases as examples in a mass education campaign (Ningdu zhongxin xianwei, 1932.7.16).

The county committee called on all district Women's Committees to immediately meet with township women's movement cadres to discuss the methods of mobilization for the campaign. It was suggested that they first hold mass meetings of women in each township, after which mass meetings in each district could be called. At the meetings, slogans were to be raised demanding a trail and the dealth penalty for the peasant who killed his wife and support for the woman who was beaten. Representatives were to be selected to go to the district government to demand that the murdered woman's husband be punished. Beyond this, women were to be mobilized to report the cases to meetings of Agricultural Laborer Unions and Poor Peasant Corps to ask them to draft resolutions in support of the beaten woman and also of policies such as the marriage regulations (Ningdu zhongxin xianwei, 1932.7.16).

Unfortunately there is no documentation on the implementation of this directive. What is striking about the Ningdu case is the strong position taken by the county party committee. Backed by such support, the women's movement in Ningdu made substantial progress. In the 1933 party recruitment drive, Ningdu's recruitment of women was among the highest in Jiangxi province (Jiangxi shengwei, 1933.9.20). By 1934, districts of Ningdu were cited as model areas as a result of the exemplary efforts of women's congress representatives in a recruitment drive for the women's militia and of the enthusiastic response of local women to the drive (*Hongse Zhonghua,* 1934.3.8).

Ningdu, however, was by no means representative. A survey of the implementation of the marriage regulations in Jiangxi province made in late 1932 revealed continuing government obstruction and prevention of divorce in a number of counties, as well as instances of arranged marriage and the taking of foster-daughters-in-law ("Jiangxi shengsu baogao," 1932.11.21). In some counties widows were prevented from receiving land in the land reform (Ganxian suweiai zhengfu, 1932.10.20), and in others they were forced to remarry quickly after the death of their husbands (*Hongse Zhonghua,* 1932.3.10). Some party organizations and members continued discrimination against women in membership and work, while others viewing women as sexual objects used them as "inducements" in various recruitment drives (*Hongse Zhonghua,* 1933.4.11; 1933.7.8). There were also instances in which youth league members forced women to sleep with them as a means of "combatting feudalism" ("Fan fengjian haishi ti fangeming zaojihui?").

Still, there can be little doubt that considerable progress was made during the period in implementing the party's program for peasant women. Although general statistics are lacking, those of the soviets in Yiyang and Hengeng counties in northeast Jiangxi, areas which had been liberated since 1927, reveal that from March 6 to June 25, 1932, there were a total of 3,783 marriages and 4,274 divorces registered (Sheng Chang, 1933: 5). Given the miniscule number of divorces outside the soviet areas, these figures are a strong indication of the success in assuring the right to divorce through the new marriage regulations. Although critical of some of the work among women in Changgang, Mao's investigation of that township revealed no restriction on divorce by late 1933. Marital relationships were more stable, and there were fewer instances of husbands abusing their wives or of extra-marital affairs (Mao, 1933.12.15:185)[3]

Aside from the women's program against feudal oppression and the struggle for its implementation, the program of most importance to women was land reform. In land redistribution, women of middle peasant, poor peasant, and agricultural laborer classes shared in the redistribution of land confiscated from landlords and rich peasants and retained ownership when they married (Chao, 1960: 28; Hsiao, 1969: 188). Land reform was viewed as a necessary condition for the future liberation of peasant women in that it established the material basis for their economic independence.

Initial land redistribution had certainly generated widespread support for the revolution, but as Philip Huang's article on Xingguo shows, it was essentially carried out from "above" with little mass participation (see also Kim, 1973: 16-17, 127). In 1933, the Land Investigtion Movement was initiated to provide a check on the thoroughness and proper redistribution of land in the first phases of agrarian reform, and to politically activate the peasants to participate in the process (Mao, 1933.8.20: 135; 1934.1.24/25: 268). The movement achieved impressive results. The Poor Peasant Corps were apparently genuinely activated for the first time through their assumption of many of the functions of the Land Committees in the earlier distribution (Lötveit, 1973: 164-165; Kim, 1973: 127). There was also substantial participation by women. Through the women's movement, a campaign was begun to encourage the active participation of women in the Poor Peasant Corps. Women's leaders also mobilized struggle for the rectification of mistakes in the initial redistribution (*Hongse Zhonghua,* 1933.9.18; Guangchang zhongxin xianwei, 1933.11.2). Enthusiasm generated in the drive affected the level of participation in other political campaigns and in the related economic construction programs.

The primary work of the women's movement in implementing economic construction programs within the soviet areas after land redistribution, centered on organizing women to participate in production, the cooperative movement, and in the establishment of day-care centers. The improvement of agricultural production was of critical importance. Agricultural output often declined for a year or two after the establishment of a soviet area due to the disruptions in the economic order caused by the changes in land ownership (Mao, 1934.1.23: 142, 145). The problem of bringing output back to pre-revolutionary levels was intensified by labor shortages which occurred as army recruitment increased. In the villages, the primary responsibility for agricultural production increasingly fell on women, a large majority of whom were untrained in the skills of ploughing and harvesting. It was essential to train women in these skills and to develop new farming methods if production was to increase (Jiangxi sheng funü lianhe hui, 1962: 3).

However, it would be erroneous to assume that the war situation was the sole motivation for bringing women into production. During the initial land redistribution the party stressed the importance of women receiving a share of the land as a precondition for their economic independence (Zhonggong zhongyang Ganbei tebie weiyuanhui, 1931.3.3). Education and propaganda for the implementation of the marriage regulations stressed that free marriage was only genuinely attainable when political liberty and a certain level of economic independence was guaranteed. Women were urged to learn production skills in order to increase the value of having received a share in the land. It was, in fact, the principle of economic liberty which underlay the heavier economic burden placed on men in cases of divorce in the 1931 marriage regulations, for it was assumed that women needed special protection until such time as they had developed the necessary labor skills to work their land (Mao, 1934.1.24/25). In addition, propaganda campaigns to end footbinding linked the practice to the restriction of economic independence (Ningdu linshi xian weiyuanhui, 1932.4.21).

These new concepts regarding economic self-sufficiency had apparently taken root among the women. Bringing women into production was not only a matter of high priority for the survival of the soviets, but it was also a response to the needs and desires of peasant women themselves, both for the improvement of their livelihood and in the furtherance of their liberation (Ningdu zhongxin xianwei, 1932.7.14; Mao, 1934.1.27: 149).

In bringing women into production, as in other aspects of social and economic policy, the party sought to raise the initiative of peasant women to change their concrete living conditions themselves. The function of the women's congresses as educational centers was central to this goal. In the congresses, the problems of production and production needs were discussed, decisions were made about the organization of ploughing, and grain growing classes and women's production teams were organized. These meetings were followed by mass meetings in the villages at which volunteers were solicited for agricultural study groups, classes and teams. In some areas, township production education committees were formed to supervise the organizing of classes for women, and the appointment of teachers, who were usually older men in the township. Classes often involved in-field training with evening discussions of methods. Enthusiasm for the classes was high. Large numbers of women often volunteered for participation at initial mass meetings ("'Sanba' jie qian Ruijin funü de huoyue").

To facilitate the entry of women into production, a campaign for the establishment of day-care centers was launched in early 1934, under general guidelines provided by the People's Committee for Internal Affairs (Neiwu renmin weiyuan, 1934.2.27). Publicity for the campaign stressed improving the livelihood of peasant women by reducing their responsibility in the raising of children and freeing them to take part in production and other activities outside the home, in improving the quality of education and care of children, and in increasing production in the soviet areas. After a trial period in Ruijin and some advanced localities, such as Xingguo, the party and congresses began establishing centers in other areas.

The process for successfully establishing the first center in Xingguo was described as follows in a provincial party communique:

> When organizing first began discussions were held in the district Women's Department and a village was chosen in which to establish the center. Next, a meeting was called to discuss the problem, followed by a mass meeting of all the women in the village. At this meeting the meaning of the day-care center was explained to each woman. After all the women understood the concept, they selected a place which was clean and of sufficient space to establish a center. Older women who were unable to engage in production were chosen to work in the center, every nine village women selecting one older woman. Children were admitted by voluntary registration of their mothers. Initially in the center there were 14-16 children, most of them of nursing age ("Xingguo de mofan tuoersuo").

After the center began functioning it was designated as a model center. Other localities were encouraged to emulate the methods used to establish it as well as its operational procedures.

The establishment of day-care centers provides a good illustration of the successful implementation of a policy designed to meet immediate needs, those of production, while simultaneously encouraging unity and local management of their own affairs on the part of peasant women. The centers were primarily under the control of local women. They selected trusted women for the work and could replace those who were ineffective. Women representatives were regularly to inspect the centers, and monthly meetings of participating parents were held to evaluate the work of the centers ("Xingguo de mofan tuoersuo"). The centers also gave new positions of responsibility to older women, who were often outside the mainstream of new activities, and helped to insure their well-being through donations of grain and collective tilling of their land by the member parents.

Mutual aid was yet another mass participation program designed to increase agricultural production, deal with the labor shortage, and improve the livelihood of the people (*Hongse Zhonghua*, 1934.7.19). Mutual aid teams were first systematically organized in early 1933 and were expanded during a membership drive in the spring of 1934. In Xingguo, for example, in February 1934, there were 318 teams with a membership of 15,615; by April, the number of teams had increased to 1,206, with 22,118 members (or about 10% of the population of the county prior to war mobilization) (*Hongse Zhonghua*, 1934.4.20).

Because of the absence of males from the villages there was naturally a larger percentage of women on the teams than men. Again, women's congresses were instrumental in developing initial membership; township labor education committees then supervised the training of women in mutual aid work. In the drive to increase mutual aid membership, Red Army family members, along with congress representatives, played a leading role. By 1934, women whose husbands, fathers or sons were army members and who were frequently among the most active women in the villages, had in some areas initiated county congresses to specifically deal with problems of economic construction and support for the Red Army. They became "model citizens" in leading the drive for mutual aid organization among peasant women, and also in arousing support for agricultural training classes, day-care centers, and other campaigns, such as the bond drive and saving campaign ("Xingguo Zhaozheng liangxian hongshu daibiao dahui tongshi wancheng").

Despite the difficulties involved in the creation of a new labor force comprised largely of women, substantial results were achieved. Large numbers of women entered agricultural production. In so doing, they took a forward step toward the attainment of economic independence and made an important contribution towards satisfying the material needs of the revolutionary war effort. The 1933 autumn harvest was betwen 20 to 25% larger than the 1932 harvest (Mao, 1933.8.20: 132). By early 1934, in many areas production had been restored to its original level, while in other areas it exceeded the pre-revolutionary level (Mao, 1934.1.24/25: 272). The use of mutual aid and ploughing teams, and other new policies such as food and consumer cooperatives, not only radically changed the patterns of social organization in the villages, but in conjunction with land redistribution, considerably improved the standard of living. These radical changes were identified by Mao as significant factors in the rise of enthusiasm among the peasants for the revolution.

It is within the context of concern for the well-being of the people and the implementation of policies to raise the quality of their lives, as well as to encourage their participation in the wielding of political power and the management of their own affairs, that the successes of army recruitment drives and the expansion of support activities for the war must be viewed. Through such policies the party was able to pursue the twin goals of overturning the old society and raising the level of consciousness and solidarity among the people. Without the implementation of such policies—from the solving of local problems, to broad campaigns waged throughout the soviet areas, such as the Land Investigation Movement, the women's struggle against feudal oppression, and the production movement—support for the war effort would have suffered greatly. For it was precisely in those areas where only war-related problems (such as expansion of the army or enlarging the transportation corps) were stressed that active support for the war effort was weakest (Mao, 1934.1.27: 148). The two aspects of revolutionary participation were mutually reinforcing and were merged into a single system of mobilization.

**Conclusion**

Following the militarist reaction of 1927, the Chinese Communist Party began to devise a revolutionary strategy which would bridge the gap between its urban origins and viewpoint and the objective realities of the Chinese revolution. The success of the new strategy, which called for the waging of a protracted struggle by establishing and maintaining armed revolutionary bases in areas where the enemy's control was comparatively weak, rested above all on gaining the support of the peasant masses for the revolution. In the early 1930s, particularly in the revolutionary base areas of south-central China, as party thinking evolved on the ways of successfully waging the revolution and war, party members came to place more importance on the role of the peasant women's movement in the revolutionary struggle. In the party's view, poor peasants and agricultural laborers were to form the crux of support for the agrarian revolution; the women of those classes in particular, were to be a major source on which to rely in consolidating the revolution in the soviet areas.

The building of a revolutionary movement among peasant women in the soviet areas was, then, part of the overall party efforts to strengthen its bonds with the peasants and eliminate the barriers created by its external origins. Like the overall movement, the women's movement was developed under a political and organizational line of championing the interests of the people and maintaining close contact with them both inside and outside the party. In concrete terms, its successes were tied to the party's development of a series of programs designed to raise the status of women while securing mass support for the social revolution and war effort. Underlying these programs were two fundamental policies: first, create the opportunity for peasant women to share in the assumption of political power, to struggle against their material and sexual oppression, and to improve the quality of their lives; and second, implement these policies through the mass participation of the women. The creation of organizational forms which developed female leadership and provided the conditions for the participation of women in revolutionary activity, and the recruitment of a large number of basic level activist cadres, who formed a link between the party and masses of women, were important factors in the success of the mobilization programs.

By 1934 a dramatic transformation had taken place in the lives of village women within the base areas. The land revolution and other programs had considerably improved the living conditions of many peasant women. The social seclusion of peasant women had been replaced by the wide-spread participation of women in politics, production, cultural affairs and the war effort. Progress had been made toward breaking down the feudal marriage system. Discrimination remained, but relative to the starting point, peasant women had made considerable progress toward gaining familial and social equality. Certainly the war situation accelerated the process of transformation in women's lives, but a basic outline for women's liberation had been created. Arising from the needs of peasant women and practical experience, this outline formed the basis for later work among rural women in the northern liberated areas,[4] and for further progress towards the liberation of women once the revolutionary victory was complete.

As a result of the changes in their lives, the peasant women in the soviet areas were united behind the revolution. Documents from 1934 give countless examples of women's activities, model women, and woman-work in specific locations which indicate a highly politicized female population, an enthusiasm for the revolutionary war effort, and the degree to which group pressure was brought to bear on those individuals who remained outside the mainstream of revolutionary activity. These reports reflect the effectiveness of mass campaigns initiated by the party in creating a political movement among peasant women. They also reveal the energy and creativity released by the peasants in revolutionary work under the leadership of a party which strove to demonstrate its concern for their well-being and to involve them in all aspects of revolutionary life.

¹Delia Davin's brief description of woman-work in the Jiangxi Period argues that disagreements among party leaders on the priorities for the women's movement were reflected in the lack of a consistent policy for women, and that while the "politicization" of women was one of the tasks of mass mobilization policies, the main direction of the movement was determined by expediency—primarily supporting the needs of the army (1976: 21-32). I have attempted to show, however, that from 1931 to 1934 there was a consistent policy for the women's movement. To be sure, war mobilization was the central task of the communist movement during these years, but the methods the party developed to accomplish this task among women centered on creating the opportunities for peasant women to struggle against material and sexual oppression, to raise their status, and to expand their roles and activities. Progress toward women's liberation and fulfilling the needs of the war were merged into a unified mobilization system.

²For example, in the summer of 1931 Meng Qing-shu (wife of Wang Ming) became Director of the Women's Committee of the Central Committee, the primary directing body for the women's movement in the party organization. She was replaced by Du Zuo-xiang in September 1931 (Meng probably left China at that time to return to Moscow with her husband) (Kuo, 1966: 45-46). In the summer of 1931, Zhang Qin-qiu was sent to the O-Yu-Wan Soviet to take charge of women's work there (Klein and Clark, 1971: 21).

³The examples given here have already been cited by Hu Chi-hsi (1975). In my opinion, Hu's article on the "sexual revolution" in the Jiangxi Period overstates the extent to which sexual morality was transformed. Nevertheless, the findings of that article collaborate the conclusions I have reached regarding party support for the implementation of the women's program and progress made in raising the status of women.

⁴See Ho Kuo-cheng (1973), The Status and Role of Women in the Chinese Communist Movement, 1946-1949 (Indiana University, unpublished dissertation) for the fullest account to date of the women's movement in the northern liberated areas. Ho's findings on party policy for women from 1946 to 1949 indicate a basic similiarity with Jiangxi policy. Ho also shows the relationship between the women's movement and mass-line leadership doctrines, first documented by Mark Selden, which as in the Jiangxi period, continued to stress the inter-relatedness of the war effort, socio-economic problems, and the transformation of women. See also Davin (1976), Chapter 1.

# The Jiangxi Period:
# A Comment on the Western Literature
### Philip C.C. Huang

Studies of the Jiangxi period, like those of present-day China, have concentrated mainly on top-level power struggles and line disputes. My purpose here is to sum up and critically assess the state of our knowledge of the period based on these studies, rather than to review individual titles.

## POWER STRUGGLES AND LINE DISPUTES

### The Party's Own Account

For years the Chinese Communist Party's own "Resolutions Concerning Certain Historical Questions" were our main source of information on intra-party struggles and line disputes in this period. Those "Resolutions," adopted under Mao Ze-dong's leadership in 1945, tell us, first of all, that from 1927 to 1934 Mao was in opposition to the Party Central most of the time, when the Central was dominated by three successive "left lines": the "first left line" under Qu Qiu-bai from August 7, 1927 to April 1928, then the "second left line" under Li Li-san, from June 11, 1930 to September 1930, and finally, the "third left line" under Wang Ming [Chen Shao-yu] and Bo Gu [Qin Bang-xian], from January 1931 to January 1935.

The heart of the dispute between Mao and Qu, and then Mao and Li, we are told, was between Mao's advocacy of building stable revolutionary base areas in the countryside and Qu's and Li's insistence on armed uprising to seize cities (Mao, 1945 "Guanyu. . .": 960-962).

The dispute between Mao and the "third left line" was more complex. The basic theoretical division was over the extent to which Chinese society was already "capitalist," and hence the extent to which the current revolution was to be directed against both feudlism (i.e. landlordism) and capitalism (i.e. against the urban bourgeoisie and the rural rich peasants). Since the communist movement was in reality based in the countryside, the dispute concerned chiefly policies toward rich peasants:

Wang Ming and Bo Gu would attack them vigorously, as they would landlords; Mao, on the other hand, would deal with rich peasants less harshly and concentrate the current struggle mainly on landlords (965-974).

This basic divergence over whether the current revolution should be anti-feudal or both anti-feudal and anti-capitalist led to other differences. Proponents of the "third left line," the "Resolutions" charged, followed too rigidly their so-called "class-line"—within the party they attacked too many of the old comrades too indiscriminately, and outside the party they attacked rich peasants and others excessively (974-975; 986-987). By insisting that the current revolution was not only anti-feudal but also anti-capitalist, they in effect also refused to acknowledge that the main content of the current struggle should be in the countryside (976-978). They were in reality profoundly suspicious of the countryside, hence of rural guerrilla warfare as well—which, according to Mao, was the main military form of a rural-based "people's war"—and insisted upon regularizing the Red Army. This kind of thinking led in turn to the faulty strategy of positional warfare in defending the base area against Chiang Kai-shek's [Jiang Jie-shi] Fifth Encirclement Campaign, an error which resulted in the forced abandonment of the base area and the subsequent Long March (977-978; 983-985).

In spite of these differences, the "Resolutions" went on to point out, proponents of the third left line and Mao worked together on the important tasks of land redistribution and the construction of new political authority in the base area (974; 990-991).

### Academic Analyses

Detailed academic analyses of these intra-party relations became possible after Hsiao Tso-liang [Xiao Zuo-liang] gained access to the Guomindang's intelligence files collected by General Chen Cheng during the extermination campaigns. The Chen Cheng materials are now available in 21 reels in microfilm. They include publications of the party, army, and government of the time, directives on varous levels, and even some internal party communications (CC; Wu, 1972; Wu, 1970). Eight full length studies have since been published on the basis of these materials, three of which, including two by Hsiao, are essentially reference works (which I will discuss briefly in the appended note). My comments here will concern mainly the five interpretive books that have been done.

As a body, the five books have served to confirm and flesh out the bones of the story given in the "Resolutions." Thus, from the first and the most comprehensive, John Rue's *Mao Tse-tung in Opposition, 1927-1935* (1966), we learn that Mao was indeed "in opposition" to the Party Central during most of this period. Already in October 1928, Li Li-san had voiced his alarm over the "danger that the base of our party may shift from the working class to the peasantry." Li, as Rue pointed out, was profundly suspicious of the "petty-bourgeois" peasants and hence of Mao's rural-based movement in the Jinggang Mountains base area (138). We also learn that Mao steadily lost more and more power to the Returned Students between 1931 and 1934. At the First National Congress of Soviet Deputies in November 1931, Mao managed to retain control over the government and military apparatus in the Central Soviet Area, but lost the control over the party apparatus to the Returned Students (248-250). Then, at the Ningdu Conference (of the Party Central) in August 1932, Mao was "forced off" the Military Committee of the Party Central by Zhou En-lai and the Returned Students, and finally replaced by Zhou as chief Political Commissar of the Red Army in May 1933. This set the stage for Zhou and the Returned Students to dominate military strategy during the Fifth Encirclement (251-253). Finally, at the Second National Congress in January-February 1934, Mao lost even his control over the government apparatus. By July 1934, his power reached such a low point that he was placed, according to Rue, "on probation" (263).

Where Rue diverged from the party's own "Resolutions" was on the question of the role of Stalin and the Comintern. The "Resolutions" chose, in 1945, to ignore the points of conflict between Mao and Moscow (although top-level internal discussions have been perfectly frank about the role of Stalin, as shown, for example, by the text of Mao's talk before an enlarged session of the Politburo in April 1956) (Mao, 1956: 24). Rue showed, however, that Mao was not only "in opposition" to the Party Central during these years, but to Stalin and the Comintern as well. The latter exerted their influence over the Chinese revolution mainly through the Returned Students: Wang Ming was the Chinese Communist Party's resident representative to the Comintern from September 1931 on (until 1937), while Pavel Mif, formerly rector of the Sun Yat-sen University where the Returned Students had studied, became in 1931 the Comintern's agent to China. Mao's struggle against the Returned Students was thus also a struggle for independence from Stalin and the Comintern.

Shanti Swarup's *A Study of the Chinese Communist Movement* (1966) helped clarify the principles at issue in the power struggles narrated by Rue. In Swarup's analysis, twentieth-century China's revolution had to be both a national revolution for independence from imperialism and a social revolution for the oppressed masses. Mao was one who understood and tried to realize this combination. The Returned Students, however, did not; their mistake was in their excessive emphasis on the social revolution, to the exclusion of a broad united front for the national revolution, hence their rigid views on class struggle and divisive policy of attacking rich peasants, and their refusal to ally with the Guomindang's Nineteenth Route Army (which had defended Shanghai courageously against the Japanese attack of early 1932) when it revolted in Fujian against Chiang Kai-shek and his policy of appeasing the Japanese (known as the Fujian Revolt—November 1933 to January 1934) (Swarup, 1966: 195-198; Rue, 1966: 261). Swarup's main contribution was to spell out the theoretical underpinnings of the line struggles in a language less rhetorical than the "Resolutions."

Subsequent studies have filled out the story further. Derek Waller's *The Kiangsi Soviet Republic: Mao and the National Congresses of 1931 and 1934* (1973) substantiated and elaborated upon some aspects of Rue's work. Waller showed that while Mao and his followers commanded a clear majority in the Central Executive Committee (of the Central Soviet Government) after the First Congress in November 1931, they lost that majority to the Returned Students in the Second Congress in 1934 (41-50; 103-108). We get from Waller basically the same picture as that given in Rue: Mao's power was steadily eroded after 1931, first in the party apparatus, then the army, and finally the government itself.

While Waller, like Rue, emphasized power relations, Ilpyong Kim's *The Politics of Chinese Communism: Kiangsi under the Soviets* (1972) was much like Swarup's in that it placed greater stress on ideological content. The book high-lighted the fact that mass mobilization was a central concern in party and government policies of this time. Where Mao and the Returned Students differed was in emphasis: Mao stressed muh more the "mass-line," or rallying the majority of the people, while the Returned Students tented to emphasize class struggle more with their "class-line," especially the struggle against rich peasants (104-117).

On the question of power relations, Kim's book performed the valuable service of reminding us that Mao and the Returned Students did not always work against each other but often worked together in "coalition." To make this point, Kim employed a triangular rather than bipolar model of the power structure in the Central Soviet Area, consisting of Mao and his followers, the Returned Students, and "party veterans" like Zhou En-lai who, in Kim's analysis, was often a mediator betwen Mao and the Returned Students. Policies, then, were frequently results of compromises and of shifting power alignments among these three major groupings of power. Since Kim did not concern himself chiefly with power relations, this framework was offered by him more as a provocative insight than as a demonstrated conclusion (56-74). But it is one that makes good sense and enables us to comprehend the statement in the "Resolutions" that Mao and the Returned Students, in spite of their differences, worked together on the important tasks of land redistribution and the building of representative local soviets.

Finally, Tgygve Lötveit's *Chinese Communism 1931-1934: Experience in Civil Government* (1973) clarified the picture of power relations in terms of the institutions of the soviet government. The two most powerful posts in the central government, we learn, were the Chair of the Central Executive Committee and the Chair of the Council of People's Commissars (Renmin weiyuanhui) (rather like the premier). Mao occupied both posts after the First Congress, but lost the latter post to Zhang Wen-tian [Luo Fu] of the Returned Students at the Second Congress (97).

Zhang Wen-tian's increased control over the soviet government, in turn, coincided with a steady "radicalization" in the government's treatment of rich peasants and counter-revolutionaries (see further discussion in the last section of this paper).

In short, thanks to the body of scholarship briefly summarized above, we need not doubt the veracity of the broad outlines of the party's own account given in the "Resolutions": there were continual power struggles between Mao and those who dominated the Party Central during the years 1927 to 1934; those struggles involved not just the pursuit of power for its own sake, but substantial differences over revolutionary principles: especially the questions of whom the social revolution should attack (landlords or landlords and rich peasants and the bourgeoisie?) and how broad a popular base the revolutionary movement should rely upon. Future studies will certainly add further refinements. Studies of power relations in the Jiangxi period will likely employ, for example, the analytical categories that have been used in studies of contemporary Chinese politics—such as "cliques" based on personal ties, "interest groups," and ideological "factions" (Starr, 1976: 479-484 sums up these approaches). There will no doubt also be further disputes [1] over specific interpretations and facts. But the broad outlines of the story have been well worked out in a rather remarkable consensus among the existing studies; they seem unlikely to be altered in any fundamental way.

## RETROSPECTIVE PEKINGOLOGY

The problem lies instead in the very nature of the information that has been accumulated. How much can we really understand about a mass movement, a social revolution, by looking at the power struggles and theoretical arguments of the top fifty individuals? What if all we knew about the American Revolution were the power relations and line disputes between Jefferson, Adams, and Hamilton? Don't we need an entirely different kind of information and analysis?

**Power Politics**

Take the First National Congress of Soviet Deputies in November 1931 for an example. That Congress summed up the preceding two years' experience in building local representative congresses (soviets), and defined guidelines for systematically constructing such soviets throughout the base areas. Those were crucial decisions in the party's efforts to root down in natural villages, to turn an urban-originated movement into a movement based on genuine peasant participation. To what extent did the movement succeed in its efforts? On which rural social groups did it come to be based? What were the sources of unity and of friction among those groups that constituted the movement's social base?

This same Congress enacted a land reform law that summed up the preceding year's experience in land reform and established guidelines for systematizing the earlier efforts and for carrying out land reform in newly liberated areas. The law was an early attempt at a systematic blueprint in the revolution's search for a strategy of social revolution in the villages. What do that law and the discussions about it tell us about the process of land reform—a process that was eventually to transform all of rural society and alter the lives of all Chinese peasants?

Rue and Waller were not interested in such questions. To Rue, the First Congress was significant only in that "the Maoists won control of the government" in their power struggle with the Returned Students (Rue, 1966: 249). And Waller, even though he summarized most of the known information about the Congress—its election regulations, proceedings and resolutions — chose to give sustained analysis only to the same issue of the "Maoists'" struggle for power against the Returned Students (Waller, 1973: 22-52).

This singular preoccupation with power politics led in Rue's case to some rather fanciful interpretations that seriously detract from an otherwise meticulous and path-breaking piece of research. To give just one example: Mao's "Investigation of Xingguo," as I showed in my article, detailed without any theoretical window dressing the preceding year's land reform, the problems and imperfections of the post land reform government, especially the predominance of lumpenproletarian elements in that government, the social and economic conditions before and after land reform, and so on; it is one of the best examples of Mao's application of his own dictum to investigate concrete conditions thoroughly. It is also the most informative document we have on real conditions in the Central Soviet Area. Rue, however, chose to interpret this report only from the perspective of a diabolical power maneuver:

> The real object of Mao's survey was to discover which landlords in the area were associated with the AB Corps and which CCP members and soviet officials had familial or business ties with the landlords and rich peasants, who were most likely to engage in counter-revolutionary activities (Rue, 1966: 223-224).

In Rue's analysis, this maneuver was somehow related to Mao's power struggle with Li Li-san at this time. But Mao nowhere mentioned any of the concerns ascribed to him by Rue. And Rue offers no other evidence for his speculations but Mao's report. When such liberties [2] are taken with the evidence, almost anything becomes possible and historical study of the Jiangxi period becomes indistinguishable from the worst of journalistic China-watching.

In Pekingology—the study of top-level power struggles and line disputes in Peking—communist parties are usually assumed to be like machines, subject to push-button dictation from the top. It follows, therefore, that the most important thing we need to know is the identity and programs of the latest top power holders, hence the spotlight on the power relations among the top leadership. Some of our China-watchers assume further that "communist" leaders are necessarily motivated above all by the search for personal power; their ideological statements are only rationalizations for their power machinations. The task of the Pekingologist is therefore to cut through all the theoretical gobbledygook to get at the really important dynamic of power struggle.

Rue and Waller, I suspect, would not have agreed with these crude notions even at the time they first conceived of their projects. Rue, especially, spoke frankly and courageously in his "Acknowledgements" of his personal admiration for Mao. But the climate of the Cold War was such that most of us came to adopt its outlook and its assumptions, even if only half-consciously. Rue and Waller, whether or not they agreed with the assumptions of crude China-watching, did in fact limit their inquiry to the power relations among fifty-odd individuals. In doing so, their work, even if unwittingly, reduced the history of the Chinese revolution to the power machinations of a few men.

## Theoretical Studies

Unlike Rue and Waller, Swarup and Kim placed their primary emphasis on ideological content. Swarup, as mentioned earlier, explained the ideological differences between Mao and the Returned Students in terms of the dual national and social character of the Chinese Revolution. He showed that Mao had a keener appreciation for the need to combine the two, while the Returned Students stressed the social revolution to the exclusion of the national revolution. Kim clarified these differences further, in terms of contrasting approaches to mass mobilization: Mao sought a broad popular base while the Returned Students emphasized narrowly interpreted class struggle.

These were important correctives to the strictly power-oriented approach that Rue had employed. In Swarup's and Kim's work, we see intra-party contentions of the Jiangxi period as principled struggles, in which serious issues of revolutionary strategy were at stake, rather than as merely power struggles for power's sake. This was an important advance over crude China-watching.

But even Swarup's and Kim's works were still burdened by a central assumption of the totalitarian model employed by Pekingologists—that "communist" societies (even with all the contending cliques, factions, and interest groups at the top), have essentially a push-button relationship between top and bottom, intent and implementation. We need not therefore ask: was what was understood at the middle and bottom ranks the same as what was declared at the top? Was what was actually accomplished the same as what was intended? How did the leadership and the people interact?

Thus, Swarup's discussion was entirely abstract and theoretical. He set out to prove that the soviet areas were seriously weakened by an excessive emphasis on social revolution which proved to be divisive. But he made his case strictly on the basis of the theoretical statements of the top leadership. He never examined the land reform of 1930 or the land investigation movement of 1933-1934, the two main instances of class struggle in the base areas. He never asked: what actually happened? This was no doubt due in part to the limitations of the material at his disposal, for he used only very little of the documents in the Chen Cheng collection. But there is no mistaking the fact that he assumed, as many of us still do, that the nature of "communist" societies is such that the declarations of the top leadership will be implemented to the letter. We need therefore only look at the lines determined at the top. It is an approach that finally reduced the Chinese revolution to the armchair theoretical exercises of a few men.

Kim's book is much more substantial and brings us closer to the real situation in the base areas by extensive use of the Chen Cheng collection. After discussing the theoretical framework for Mao's ideas on mass mobilization in the language of political science,[3] and the differences between Mao and the Returned Students, Kim went on to provide a description of the pattern of land reform (Kim, 1973: 118-126), the structure of the mass organizations (126-135), the land investigation movement (135-143), and the structure of the township and district soviets (162-178).

However, Kim's work still suffered from the same assumption with which Swarup worked. On the land investigation movement, for example, Kim simply summarized the declared intent—a mass movement to systematically assess the results of the earlier land reform, to carry through the social revolution where it had not been thoroughly implemented; a movement behind which the local soviets and mass organizations were to be mobilized—and then concluded that Mao intended the movement to be a part of the larger efforts at mass moblization. He did not ask: how did the movement actually work? How much actual class struggle was there?—an important question that would give us at once a sense of the real scale of the movement and, at the same time, a clear indication of how thorough the earlier land revolution had been. This was a question that Lötveit, who worked with a much keener sensitivity to the relationship between theory and practice, policy and implementation, immediately asked (see discussion below). The effect of Kim's approach, like Swarup's, is to suggest that policy declarations at the top were the same as accomplished fact. The irony is that Kim should have worked with such an assumption when his focus was on the theory of mass participation.

The roots of this disregard for the practical context lie perhaps in part in the nature of the material with which all of us work. Party documents are commonly written from the standpoint that "the correctness and incorrectness of ideological and political line decide everything." They tend therefore to be extremely abstract and theoretical, taking great pains to show how the correct line was arrived at "scientifically." After months and years of reading such documents, some of us might even unwittingly absorb the same outlook; we certainly learn that it is much easier to study just the design of party policy than to obtain concrete information on what actually happened.

We must not forget, however, that in the Chinese context, such abstract statements take for granted some knowledge of the trials and errors, pilot experiments, lengthy discussions and summing-ups, deviations right and left, that accompany the formulation of every line. The claim to "scientific" analysis, therefore, is understood in the context of a constant interplay between theoretical formulation and practical implementation. We the researchers, however, can count on no such knowledge of the practical context. Our task must instead be first of all to reconstruct that concrete context—the actual problems to which the line was addressed, the difficulties encountered in implementation, the relationship between intent and actual result. To fail to do so, as I shall show in the next section, is often to be completely mistaken about what actually happened. It is also to fall into the trap of Pekingology and reduce Chinese society to the power machinations and theoretical exercises of a few individuals.

## NEW DIRECTIONS

### Theory and Practice

Trygve Lötveit's book finally broke out of the confines of Pekingological assumptions. Because of its common sense questioning of how theory was rendered into practice, policy into implementation, Lötveit managed to show for the first time the actual consequences of Mao and the Returned Students' disputes over policies for the base areas. Thus, Zhang Wen-tian's rise in the Central Government after the Second Congress meant a sharp turn toward harsher treatment of (former) landlords and rich peasants in the base areas. Mao had tried in October 1933, after the first phase of the Land Investigation Movement, to mitigate the class struggle advocated by the Returned Students by clarifying the criteria for class classification and by enlarging the scope allowed for middle peasant status (permitting up to 15% of total income to be from exploitative sources) and for rich peasant status (so that any household in which there was one member who worked at least four months of the year would be classified as rich peasant rather than landlord). But Mao's efforts were rebuked by the Party Central in January 1934, and Zhang, as the new Chair of the Council of People's commissars, called for radicalization in March. The result was that almost all rich peasants were drafted into labor brigades and their property expropriated. At the same time, an indiscriminate attack was launched against cadres of rich peasant and landlord backgrounds (Lötveit, 1973: 172-184).

There was a parallel development in judicial policies. Lötveit demonstrated convincingly that Zhang's ascendance in the soviet government and his call for radicalization changed a judicial system that had been relatively lenient and standardized into virtual Red Terror. Local judicial bodies were given sanction to conduct executions on their own authority; mass opinions were allowed a decisive voice in the sentencing of counter-revolutionaries; revolutionary considerations (and, I might add, the pressures of the Fifth Encirclement) came to prevail completely over any semblance of legality. Lötveit made his case not only with evidence from governmental directives but also with material from specific individual cases (Lötveit, 1973: 119-144).

This kind of analysis, like Lynda Bell's article on agricultural workers, carries far more substance than analyses of power struggles or abstract theories, for it shows clearly the actual consequences of intra-party disputes.

This practice-conscious approach enabled Lötveit to make other important contributions. Unlike Kim's abstract treatment of the Land Investigation Movement, for example, Lötveit gave us immediately a sense of the actual scale of the movement in the Central Soviet Area: the movement uncovered in the summer of 1933 a total of some 7,000 landlords and 6,600 rich peasants who had escaped proper classification earlier (Lötveit, 1973: 168). If we assume that approximately 3% of the population in the area were landlords, there would have been 90,000 landlords (among the population of 3 million). We thus get an immediate gauge of the extent and actual results of the movement (and, coincidentally, also a measure of how thorough the earlier land reform had been).

Lötveit's main contribution, of course, is what he set out to do: to analyze the structure and functioning of the institutions of the soviet government. On this subject—the workings of the township, district, county, province, and central soviets—his study has been restricted only by the limitations in the documentary information; it is unlikely to be surpassed in the years to come. We need more work of this kind.

I began my own research into Xingguo county with the similar notion that the stated word must be analyzed in conjunction with what actually happened. My research led me to the surprising conclusion that, in the first few years after 1927, the revolutionary movement acquired a strongly bandit-like social composition, as the radical intellectuals found their most ready allies in the lumpenproletariat rather than the poor peasants. This problem did not, however, make its way into top-level theoretical discussions of the time, in part, no doubt, because the leadership were understandably sensitive to the charge that the movement merely consisted of "Red bandits," and in part because there was little room in Marxist-Leninist theory for the role of the lumpenproletariat in the main argument of the day that focussed on whether the revolution should be primarily anti-feudal or both anti-feudal and anti-capitalist. The problem has therefore been overlooked in all studies of the Jiangxi period. But it was in reality the principal deviant tendency at least until 1931, and the reality of the problem has been preserved in such documents as Mao's "Investigation of Xingguo" and Chen Qi-han's reminiscences.

To give another example of how top-level theoretical documents can be extremely misleading: much has been written about the differences between Mao and Li Li-san in 1930 on the question of rich peasants (Rue, 1966: 164-166; Hsiao, 1969: 3-16; 127-130). I myself have shown that Mao had been convinced at least since the Jinggang days that rich peasants must be treated with moderation in order to avoid alienating all the "intermediate classes" (especially middle peasants) (Huang, 1975). Li Li-san, for his part, would have been even more moderate than Mao and would have left the rich peasants largely untouched. The line between Mao and Li Li-san was a fine one. However, these fine points mattered little when it came to the actual implementation of the land reform in March 1930. In the memory of Chen Qi-han, who was acting in the field as the Xingguo county party committee secretary, the orders he received amounted to simply: "Divide! Fast!" And the land reform in Xingguo was in fact violent and radical toward rich peasants, not so much because of any strategy determined at the top, but rather because of the realities of local conditions: the Xingguo countryside had been militarily polarized along class lines, with landlords and rich peasants organizing to fight the communists. Under such conditions, land reform became very violent.

Such evidence suggests that we must never take for granted that what was declared at the top levels was the same as what actually happened—a common sense observation, it seems to me, that would have guided our work long ago had it not been for the peculiar ideological burdens of our field.

## Leadership and Social Base

An increased awareness of the relationship between theory and practice should lead us to question how the top levels of the party interacted with the lower levels and how the leadership interacted with its social base. The three articles in this volume were intended to be preliminary explorations of the question: how did the radical intellectuals from the cities interact with different social groups in the countryside—the lumpenproletariat, rich, middle and poor peasants, agricultural workers, and women? The tentative conclusion here is that the movement, in spite of the strong deviant tendencies toward a bandit-like social composition (discussed in my article) and later toward an unrealistic and narrow reliance on agricultural workers (analyzed in Lynda Bell's article), came to be based on the largest social groups in the countryside: poor peasant men and women. My article on Xingguo suggests that land reform and the construction of local soviets were crucial in this process of forging a link between urban intellectuals and poor peasants. Lynda Bell's article shows that the Party's efforts at mass mobilization took hold only when the leadership moved away from a doctrinaire emphasis on "proletarian leadership." Kathy Walker's suggests that the party made serious efforts to activate peasant women around women's issues as well as larger revolutionary programs, even before the demands of war made women's involvement in production and leadership not just a desired goal but the necessary fact.[4] We need to know much more about how these processes actually worked and about the problems encountered. We also need to know more about the roles of other social groups such as artisans and petty merchants.

Another question that needs to be answered is: what were the areas of unity and of friction beteen the different social groups and classes that comprised the movement? How were those relationships reflected in the leadership structure? The material here can only offer a very preliminary and rather imprecise answer. The central "contradiction" in the movement of the time was between urban intellectuals and rural peasants, and major party struggles reflected this basic contradiction. Seen in this perspective, the three left lines might be understood as representing those elements among the urban intellectuals who were distrustful of the countryside and of peasants—hence as Lynda Bell shows, their insistence on exaggerating the extent of capitalist development in China and their rigid interpretation of "proletarian leadership" and the "class-line." At bottom, I suspect, such emphases reflected the basic prejudices that urbanites harbored toward "backward" villages. A lack of practical experience in the villages also led individuals like Wang Ming to assign, from the distance of Moscow, a totally unrealistic role to the tiny minority who were agricultural workers in Jiangxi.

Yet, the urban orientation of individuals like Wang Ming did not hinder them from joining forces with Mao to purge the party of its heavy reliance on the lumpenproletariat, and to penetrate the natural villages through land reform and the building of local soviets. They also worked readily with Mao in efforts to liberate the revolutionary energies of rural women.

There were thus important areas of unity as well as of friction between the urban oriented radical intellectuals and the peasant based movement. We need to know much more about how the relationships between those two basic social components of the revolution developed and changed, and how those relationships related to other "contradictions" such as those between men and women, workers and peasants, merchants and peasants, and so on. Then, perhaps, we shall be able to place top-level struggles into their larger societal context. More important, we shall be able to understand the Chinese Revolution for what it was: a gigantic social movement that first took definite shape in the Jiangxi period.

## A Note on Sources

Hsiao Tso-liang's two pioneering volumes, *Power Relations in the Communist Movement, 1930-1934: A Study of Documents* (1961) and *The Land Revolution in China, 1930-1934: A Study of Documents* (1969) remain useful as convenient references on those subjects. Cao Bo-yi's *Jiangxi suweiai zhi jianli ji qi bengkui* (The establishment of the Jiangxi Soviet and its disintegration) (1969) details and chronicles most important external features of the subject: the congresses, the encirclement campaigns, the government organs, available budgetary information, figures on military recruitment, and so on. The abundant quotes make it a good introductory guide to the materials in the basic Chen Cheng collection.

We have, in addition, several convenient collections and bibliographic aids. The appendices to the twelve volume *Chūgoku kyōsantōshi shiryō shū* (Collection of source materials on the history of the Chinese Communist Party) (Nihon kokusai mondai kenkyūjo, 1970-1974) is the most comprehensive chronological listing of principal documents on party history, and a good starting point for anyone working on the subject. The ten volume Japanese edited *Mao Ze-dong ji* (1972) contains in readily usable form not only most of Mao's writings in their earliest editions but also many of the important directives of the Central Soviet Government. The annotated bibliographic guide to the Chen Cheng collection compiled by Wu Tien-wei (1972) some years ago remains in manuscript form at the Harvard Yenching Library; I myself have had to make do with the unannotated listing in "Kōsei sobieto kankei shiryō mokuroku" (1963).

[1] William Dorrill, in an article on "The Fukien [Fujian] Rebellion and the CCP," has questioned whether there really were any differences between Mao and the Party Central over the Fujian rebels (Dorrill, 1969). More recently, Dorrill has further argued that Mao did not lose his power over the army at the Ningdu Conference—the "Resolutions" only suggested that Mao did in order to absolve him of any responsibility for the defeat the movement suffered in the Fifth Encirclement, and hence establish Mao's claim to "infallibility" (Dorrill, 1974).

Peter Donovan has now added his voice to Dorrill's to argue that there were no real differences between Mao and the Party Central over military strategy (Donovan, 1976: 11-13, 15, 90-96).

The case seems to me a weak one, however. Donovan himself shows clearly that there were fundamental issues of strategy at stake in the struggle at the Ningdu conference (90-92). Yet, he somehow manages to conclude a page later that the real differences were matters of "style and experience" (93). Two pages later, Donovan once more offers the same analysis of the Ningdu conference as that given by Rue and Waller (96). This rather forced and ambivalent argument seems to me to detract from an otherwise sound paper showing the increased politicization of the Red Army during the years 1931-1934. Donovan's research is especially thorough on the identities of the top personnel of the numerous Army Corps that made up the Red Army of this period.

[2] Another example is Rue's argument that Liu Di, in the Futian Incident, was actually trapped into revolting by Mao who was looking for an opportunity for further purges (Rue, 1966: 232). As Ronald Suleski has shown in his brief article on the Futian Incident, this is much too fanciful and diabolical an interpretation (Suleski, 1968).

[3] Mao's class analysis, for example, becomes in Kim's reinterpretation "the heart of his theory of organization," for it established "collective identity among the peasant masses," and "collective identity," in the organization theory of Theodore Caplow, is one basic prerequisite for a "formal organization" (Kim, 1973: 21).

[4] Hu Chi-hsi's narrowly focussed study of sexual mores in the soviet areas (Hu, 1974) gives much weight to examples of "free sex" excesses and confirms that very great changes indeed had been wrought by the revolution.

# REFERENCES

*Chinese and Japanese Sources*

CC stands for the 21 reels of microfilm of materials in the Chen Cheng collection (Shi-sou ziliaoshi) in Taiwan. Some documents from this collection are not dated in full (that is, sometimes the year or even the entire date is missing). The Hoover Institution, in several cases, has attempted to date such documents. In other cases, through mention of particular documents in other places, we have estimated some dates. All such questionable dates are indicated with the use of question marks in our citations.

BA ZHEN (1932) "Jinian 'sanba' yu funü gongzuo yingyou de zhuanbian" (Celebrating March 8th and changes that should be made in woman-work). Hongse Zhonghua (Red China) 12 (March 2). CC Reel 16

CAO BO-YI (1969) Jiangxi suweiai zhi jianli ji qi bengkui (The rise and fall of the Jiangxi Soviet, 1931-1934). Taibei: Institute of East Asian Studies, National "Zhengzhi" University.

CHANG HAN (1930a) "Zuzhi gunong gonghui—Wanxian gunong de shenghuo jiqi douzheng" (Organizing agricultural laborer unions—the life of agricultural laborers in Wanxian and their struggle). Hongqi (Red flag) 114 (June 28).
(1930b) "Wanxian gunong de douzheng gangling" (Struggle outline of Wanxian agricultural laborers). Hongqi (Red flag) 114 (June 28).

CHEN QI-HAN (1958) "Xingguo de chuqi geming douzheng" (The early revolutionary struggle in Xingguo) in Xinghuo liaoyuan (Sparks that started the prairie fire), Vol. I: 407-416. Beijing: Renmin wenxue chubanshe.

CHEN ZHENG-MO (1935) Gesheng nonggong guyong xiguan ji

xugong zhuangkuang (The hiring practices and the supply of and demand for hired agricultural labor in different provinces). Nanjing: Zhongshan wenhua jiaoyu guan.

Chifei jimi wenjian huibian (A collection of red bandit secret documents). CC Reel 20.

DENG YING-CHAO (1933) "Shiji wei gonggu yu jiaqiang wuchanjieji lingdaoquan er douzheng de jiantao" (Review of the struggle to realize the consolidation and strengthening of the leadership power of the proletariat). Douzheng (Struggle) 1 (February 4). CC Reel 18.
(1932) "Xinde lingdao fangshi he chedi zhuanbian" (New leadership methods and thorough change). Dang de jianshe (Party construction) 1 (June 5): 3-11. CC Reel 17.

Diyici guonei geming zhanzheng shiqi de nongmin yundong (The peasant movement during the period of the First Revolutionary Civil War) (1953) Beijing: Renmin chubanshe.

Diyici quanguo suweiai dahui zhuxituan he Zhonghua suweiai gongheguo zhongyang zhixing weiyuanhui (The Presidium of the First National Congress of Soviet Deputies and the Central Executive Committee of the Soviet Republic of China) (1931.12.1) "Zhonghua suweiai gongheguo tudi fa" (Land Law of the Chinese Soviet Republic). Cited and translated in Hsiao (1969), Doc. 34: 52-55, 186-191.

Fandong wenjian huibian (A collection of reactionary documents). CC Reel 19.

"Fan fengjian haishi ti fangeming zao jihui?" (Combating feudalism or creating opportunities for the counter-revolution?) (1932) Qingnian shihua (True words of youth) 11 (February 25). CC Reel 18.

Gannan tewei ji Xingguo xianwei tongzhi (Communique from the south Jiangxi special committee and the Xingguo county committee) (1931.6.17) "Guanyu Gan xi-nan tequwei ji gelu fenquwei chexiao wenti" (On the termination of the western and southern Jiangxi special area committee and the various district branch committees).

CC Reel 14.

Ganxian suweiai zhengfu (Ganxian soviet government) (1932.10.20) "Wei gaizheng guoqu dui funü gongzuo hushi wenti" (On rectifying the problem of neglecting woman-work in the past). CC Reel 4.

"Geming funü de mofan" (Models for revolutionary women) (1934) Hongse Zhonghua (Red China) 163 (March 27). CC Reel 17.

Gongchan guoji dongfangbu (Comintern Far East Department) (1930.11.20) "Suweiai quyu tudi nongmin wenti jueyian caoan" (Draft resolutions on the land and peasant questions in the soviet areas). CC Reel 17.

Gonglue xian funü shenghuo gaishan weiyuanhui (Committee for the improvement of women's living conditions in Gonglue county) (1931.7.8 [?]) "Gonglue xian gequ diyici funü shenghuo gaishan weiyuanhui zhuren lianxi huiyi jueyian" (Resolutions of the first joint conference of the heads of the district committees for the improvement of women's living conditions of Gonglue county). CC Reel 4

Guangchang zhongxin xianwei (Guangchang county core committee) (1933.11.2 [?]) "Gequ funübuzhang lianxi huiyi jueyi" (Resolutions of the joint meeting of the heads of the district women's departments of Guangchang county). CC Reel 4.

Guoji (Comintern) (1931.2.18) "Duiyu Zhongguo nongmin wenti jueyian" (Resolutions on the Chinese peasant question). Reprinted in Chifei jimi wenjian huibian, Book 3, part 4.

Guoji gunong weiyuanhui mishuchu (Secretariat of the Comintern agricultural laborer committee) (1931.12) "Guanyu Zhongguo gunong gonghui de jueyian" (Resolutions on China's agricultural laborer unions). CC Reel 12.

HARA MASARU (1935) "Chūgoku sobieto ni okeru hinnō oyobi kōnō no soshiki to sono tōsō kōryō" (The organizations of the poor peasants and agricultural laborers in the Chinese soviet areas and their programs of struggle). Mantetsu chōsa geppō 15, 5 (May 1935): 137-148.

HATANO KENICHI (ed.) (1961) Shiryō shūsei: Chūgoku kyōsantō shi (Collection of historical materials: History of the communist party of China), Vol. IV. Tokyo: Jiji tsūshin sha.

HE ZHONG-REN (1953) "Dierci guonei geming zhanzheng shiqi geming genjudi de jiceng zhengquan jianshe" (The construction of basic level political organs in the revolutionary base areas at the time of the Second Revolutionary Civil War) in Shixue shuangzhoukan she (ed.) (1956) Dierci guonei geming zhanzheng shiqi shishi luncong (Collection of essays on the historical events of the Second Revolutionary Civil War). Beijing: Sanlian.

Hongse Zhonghua (Red China) (Organ of the Provisional Central Government of the Soviet Republic of China) Nos. 1 to 243 (Dec. 11, 1931 to Oct. 20, 1934). CC Reels 16 and 17.

Jiangxi sheng funü lianhe hui (ed.) (Women's liaison committee of Jiangxi Province) (1962) in Jiangxi funü geming douzheng gushi (Reminiscences of the revolutionary struggles of Jiangxi women). Beijing: Zhongguo funü zazhishe.

"Jiangxi shengsu baogao" (Jiangxi provincial soviet report) (1932) Hongse Zhonghua (Red China) 4 (November 21). CC Reel 16.

Jiangxi shengwei (Jiangxi provincial party committee) (1933.10.11) "Zhaoji quansheng nügong nongfu daibiao huiyi de jueding" (The decision to summon the provincial congress of women workers and peasant women). CC Reel 4.

(1933.9.20) "Dang de zuzhi zhuangkuang" (The condition of the party's organization). CC Reel 2.

(1933.9) "Chatian yundong de gaikuang" (The general situation of the land investigation movement). CC Reel 17.

"Kōsei sobieto kankei shiryō mokuroku" (Catalogue of sources pertaining to the Jiangxi soviet) (1963) Kindai Chūgoku kenkyū senta ihō (Bulletin of the Center for Modern Chinese Studies) 3 (September): 1-30.

LIU JUN-XIU (1951) "Jiangxi nongcun jieji guanxi yu ge jieceng tudi zhanyou de chubu yanjiu" (Preliminary investigations into Jiangxi's rural class relations and land ownership of the different classes) in Xinqu tudi gaige qian de nongcun (Villages in the newly liberated areas before land reform): 40-53. Beijing: Renmin chubanshe.

LUO MAI (1933) "Ba tiba xin de ganbu dangzuo zuzhi shang de zhandou renwu" (Treat the promoting of new cadres as the fighting task of our organizing work) (1933) Douzheng (Struggle) 25 (September 5). CC Reel 18.

MAO ZE-DONG (1972) Mao Ze-dong ji (Collected works of Mao Ze-dong). 10 vols. Tokyo: Hokubōsha.

(1964) Mao Ze-dong xuanji (Selected works of Mao Ze-dong). Beijing: Renmin chubanshe.

(1945) "Guanyu ruogan lishi wenti de jueyi" (Resolutions concerning certain historical questions). Mao (1964): 955-1002.

(1934.4.10) "Xiangsu zenyang gongzuo?" (How is the township soviet to do its work?) in Mao (1972), Vol. IV 337-354.

(1934.1.24/25) "Zhonghua suweiai gongheguo zhongyang zhixing weiyuanhui yu renmin weiyuanhui dui dierci quanguo suweiai daibiao dahui de baogao" (Report of the Chinese Soviet Republic's Central Executive Committee and Council of People's Commissars to the Second National Congress of Soviet Deputies) in Mao (1972), Vol. IV: 219-282. Translated in Yakhontoff (1934): 249-283.

(1933.12.15) "Changgang xiang diaocha" (Investigation of Changgang township) in Mao (1972), Vol. IV: 125-174.

(1933.9.6) "Jinnian de xuanju" (This year's election) in Mao (1972), Vol. IV: 13-22.

(1933.8) "Chatian yundong de chubu zongjie" (Preliminary summing-up of the land investigation movement) in Mao (1972), Vol. III: 341-356. Cited and translated by Hsiao (1969), Doc. 84: 95-97, 236-254.

(1933.7.15) "Pinnongtuan zuzhi yu gongzuo dagang" (Outline of the organization and work of the poor peasant corps) in Mao (1972), Vol. III: 283-290.

(1933.6) "Zenyang fenxi jieji" (How to analyze the classes) in Mao (1972), Vol. III: 265-268.

(1933) "Caixi xiang diaocha" (Investigation of Caixi township) in Mao (1972), Vol. IV: 175-198.

(1932.9.20) "Guanyu jixu gaizao difang suweiai de wenti" (On the problem of continuing reconstruction of the local soviets) in Mao (1972), Vol. III: 131-133.

(1931.1.26) "Xingguo diaocha" (Investigation of Xingguo) in Mao (1972), Vol. II: 185-252.

(1930.11.15) "Fenqing he chuzu wenti" (The question of dividing up cropland and of land renting) in Mao (1972), Vol. II: 165-172.

(1929.12) "Zhongguo gongchandang hongjun disijun dijiuci daibiao dahui jueyian" (Resolutions of the Ninth Congress of the Chinese Communist Party of the Fourth Army of the Red Army) in Mao (1972), Vol. II: 77-125.

(1928.12) "Jinggangshan qianwei dui zhongyang de baogao" (Report of the Jinggangshan front committee to the central) in Mao (1972), Vol. II: 25-66.

(1927.3.28) "Hunan nongmin yundong kaocha baogao" (Report on an investigation of the peasant movement in Hunan) in Mao (1972), Vol. I: 207-249.

(1926) "Zhongguo shehui ge jieji de fenxi" (Analysis of classes in Chinese society) in Mao (1972), Vol. I: 161-173.

MORI MASAO (1975) "Jūhachi-nijūsseiki no kōseishō nōson ni okeru shasō, gisō ni tsuite no ichi kentō" (A study of community granaries and charitable granaries in the villages of Jiangxi province from the 18th to the 20th century). Tōyōshi kenkyū 33, 4 (March): 60-98.

Neiwu renmin weiyuan (People's committee for internal affairs) (1934) "Tuoersuo zuzhi tiaoli" (Instructions for organizing day-care centers). Hongse Zhonghua (Red China) 155 (February 27). CC Reel 17.

Ningdu linshi xian weiyuanhui (Provisional county committee of Ningdu) (1932.4.21 [?]) "Ningdu xian funü yundong jihua" (Work plan for the women's movement of Ningdu county). CC Reel 4.

Nihon Kokusai Mondai Kenkyūjo Chūgoku Bukai (ed.) (1970-1974) Chūgoku kyōsantōshi shiryō shū (Collection of source materials on the history of the Chinese Communist Party). 12 vols. Tokyo: Keisō shobō.

Nindu xianwei (Ningdu county party committee) (1932.6.10) "Fazhan dang de zuzhi jiaqiang dang de lingdao" (Expanding the party organization and strengthening party leadership). CC Reel 2.

(1932.1.18) "Gezhong gongnong jieji de jieshi ji qi duixiang" (An explanation of the various worker-peasant classes and their referents). CC Reel 17.

Ningdu zhongxin xianwei (Ningdu county core party committee) (1932.7.16 [?]) "Fadong laodong funü fandui fengjian yapo de douzheng" (Mobilize the struggle of laboring women against feudal oppression). CC Reel 4.

(1932.7.14 [?]) "Fadong Gandong laodong funü douzheng de gangling he fangshi" (The principles and methods for mobilizing the laboring women's struggle in eastern Jiangxi). CC Reel 4.

(1932.7.10) "Zhonggong Ningdu zhongxin xianwei diyici kuodahui jueyi" (Resolutions of the first enlarged session of the party core committee of Ningdu county). CC Reel 15.

(1932.4.5 [?]) "Guanyu kaiban diyiqi shixiban" (On the opening of the first session of training classes). CC Reel 3.

"Pengpeng bobo de Zhongguo suweiai yundong" (The flourishing

Chinese soviet movement) (1931) Hongqi zhoubao (Red flag weekly) 24 (November 27): 28-50.

RUAN XIAO-XIAN (1930) "Zenyang lai fandui funong" (How to oppose rich peasants). Hongqi (Red flag) 99 (May 7).

" 'San ba' jie qian Ruijin funü de huoyue" (The activities of women in Ruijin before the March 8th celebration) (1934). Hongse Zhonghua 155 (February 27). CC Reel 17.

"Shaogong beilu zhiwei qing fu shuji lianxi weiyuanhui jueyian" (Resolutions of the conference of young women secretaries of the North Jiangxi branch of the Communist Youth Corps) (1931.3). CC Reel 20.

SHENG CHANG (1933) "Chiqu zhong de nannü guanxi" (The relations between men and women in the red areas). Guowen zhoubao (The China weekly review) 10 (August 14).

Sifa xingzhengbu diaochaju (ed.) (Bureau of Investigation, Ministry of Justice) (1961) Gongfei de funü yundong (The communist bandits' women's movement). Taibei: Diaochaju.

"Suweiai zhanxing xuanjufa" (Provisional soviet election law) (1933.8.9) in Mao (1972), Vol. III: 309-323.

"Taihe xian chise zong gonghui gequ weiyuanzhang lianxi huiyi jueyian" (Resolutions of the conference of all district-level chairpersons of the red labor union of Taihe county) (1931.4.26). CC Reel 12.

Taihe xian gongnongbing dierci daibiao dahui (Second congress of workers, peasants and soldiers of Taihe county) (1930.9.2) "Gunong wenti caoan" (Draft resolutions on the agricultural laborer question). Reprinted in Chifei jimi wenjian huibian, Book 4, A.III.

WANG MING (1930) "Weishemma bu zuzhi gunong gonghui?" (Why are we not organizing agricultural laborer unions?) Hongqi (Red flag) 102, 103, 104 (May 17, 21, 24).

WANG YU-QUAN (1935) "Zhongguo nongcun guyong laodong wenti" (The question of Chinese rural hired labor). Guowen zhoubao (The China weekly review) 12, 15 (April 22): 1-8 (s.p.).

WU MEI (1930a) "Suweiai qu de nongfu gongzuo" (Peasant woman-work in the soviet areas). Hongqi (Red flag) 95 (April 26).

(1930b) "Zhunbei 'wuyi' zhong de funü gongzuo" (Prepare for the woman-work on the occasion of "May 1st"). Hongqi (Red flag) 93 (April 14).

Xiang-E-Gan sheng weiyuanhui (Hunan-Hubei-Jiangxi provincial committee) (1932.1.14) "Funü yundong gongzuo dagang" (Work plan for the women's movement) in Sifa xingzhengbu diaochaju (ed.) (1961): 22.

"Xingguo de mofan tuoersuo" (Xingguo's model day-care centers) (1934) Shengwei tongxun ([Jiangxi] provincial committee communique) 86 (April 19). CC Reel 17.

Xingguo xianwei (Xingguo county party committee) (1931.6.16) (Directive with no title), in "Chatian yundong de gaikuang" (General conditions of the land investigation movement), 1933.9. CC Reel 17.

"Xingguo Zhaozheng liangxian hongshu daibiao dahui tongshi wancheng" (The simultaneous completion of the congresses of Red Army dependents of Xingguo and Zhaozheng counties). Hongse Zhonghua 229 (Sept. 4). CC Reel 17.

"Xuanju weiyuanhui de gongzuo xize" (Regulations on the work of the election committees) (1931.12) in Mao (1972), Vol. III: 83-87.

"Xuexi Xingguo Fantai qu fazhan nü dangyuan mofan" (Learn from Xingguo's Fantai district's model work in increasing women party members) (1934) Shengwei tongxun ([Jiangxi] provincial committee communique) 83 (April 7). CC Reel 17.

YEN ZHONG-PING et al. (eds.) (1955) Zhongguo jindai jingji shi tongji ziliao xuanji (Selections from statistical source materials in modern Chinese economic history). Beijing: Kexue chubanshe.

YI-LAN (pseud.) (1958) "Chen Zan-xian" in Hongse fengbao (The red windstorm), Vol. III: 5-15. Jiangxi: Jiangxi renmin chubanshe.

ZHANG YOU-YI (ed.) (1957) Zhongguo jindai nongye shi ziliao (Source materials on China's modern agricultural history). Vol. II, 1912-1927. Beijing: Sanlian shudian.

Zhonggong Gan xi-nan tequ weiyuanhui (Chinese Communist Party western and southern Jiangxi special area committee) (n.d., 1931 [?]) "Pinnonghui zuzhifa ji qi renwu" (How to organize the poor peasant association and its tasks) in Chifei jimi wenjian huibian, Book 2.

Zhonggong Jiangxi suqu shengwei (Jiangxi soviet area provincial party committee) (1931.12) "Kuoda huiyi zhengzhi jueyian" (Political resolutions of the enlarged plenary session). CC Reel 14.

Zhonggong suqu zhongyangju (Chinese Communist Party Central Soviet Bureau) (1932.2.20 [?]) "Laodong funü daibiao huiyi zuzhi he gongzuo dagang" (Outline for the organization and work of the laboring women's congresses). CC Reel 4.

(1931.11) "Suqu gonghui yundong jueyian: suqudang diyici daibiao dahui tongguo" (Resolutions on the soviet areas' labor union movement: passed by the First Soviet Areas' Party Congress). CC Reel 12.

(1931.2.26) "Zhunbei 'sanba' jinianjie bing gaizheng funü gongzuo zhong de cuowu" (Prepare for the March 8th commemorative holiday and rectify mistakes in woman-work). CC Reel 4.

(1931.2.8) "Tudi wenti yu fan funong celue" (The land question and anti-rich peasant tactics) as cited in Hsiao (1969), Doc. 25: 38-39.

Zhonggong suqu zhongyangju zuzhibu (Chinese Communist Party soviet areas' Central Bureau organization department)(1932.9.10)"Ningdu canzhan gongzuo de jianyue" (Review of Ningdu's war effort) in Dang de jianshe (Party construction) 4: 10-16, CC Reel 17.

(1932.6.12) "Fazhan dang he gaizao dang de gongzuo dagang" (An outline for the work of expanding and reconstructing the party) in Dang de jianshe (Party construction) 2. CC Reel 17.

Zhonggong zhongyang ganbei tebie weiyuanhui (Special committee for north Jiangxi of the Central Committee of the Chinese Communist Party) (1931.3.3) "Funü gongzuo jihua" (Plan for woman-work). CC Reel 20.

Zhonggong zhongyang weiyuanhui (Central Committee of the Chinese Communist Party) (1930.4.5) "Wuyue gongzuo yu funü yundong" (Work in May and the women's movement). CC Reel 4.

(1929.12.1) "Guanyu nügong nongfu yundong de gongzuo luxian" (On the line for work on the women workers and peasant women's movement) in Sifa xingzhengbu diaochaju (ed.) (1961): 35-36.

"Zhongguo gongchandang diliuci quanguo daibiao dahui guanyu nongmin yundong jueyian" (Resolution of the Sixth National Congress of the Chinese Communist Party on the peasant movement) (1928.9) as cited and translated in Brandt, Schwartz and Fairbank (1966):156-165.

"Zhongguo gongchandang diliuci quanguo daibiao dahui tudi wenti jueyian" (Resolution of the Sixth National Congress of the Chinese Communist Party on the land question ) (1928.7) as cited in Zhang You-yi (1957): 433.

"Zhongguo nongye gongren gonghui dengjibiao" (Chinese rural workers' union registration form) (n.d.). CC Reel 12.

"Zhonghua suweiai gongheguo de xuanju xize" (Election regulations of the Soviet Republic of China) (1931.11) in Mao (1972), Vol. III: 27-37.

"Zhonghua suweiai gongheguo linshi zhongyang zhengfu renmin weiyuanhui xunling, dishiyihao—shixing guangfan shenru de chatian yundong" (Instruction No. 11 of the council of people's commissars of the provisional central government of the Chinese Soviet Republic—launching an extensive and intensive land investigation movement) (1933.6.1) as printed in Hongse Zhonghua (Red China) 87 (June 20, 1933). Cited and translated by Hsiao (1969), Doc. 60:79-81, 198-202.

Zhonghua suweiai quyu zhongyang geming junshi weiyuanhui zong zhengzhibu (General political department of the Chinese soviet areas' central revolutionary military council) (1931.2a) "Gunong gonghui zhanxing zhangcheng" (Provisional regulations for the agricultural laborer union) in Chifei jimi wenjian huibian, Book 2.

(1931.2b) "Pinnonghui zhangcheng" (Regulations for the poor peasant association) in Fandong wenjian huibian, Vol. I, Book 4.

ZHONG PING (1933) "Bosheng cheng qu de chatian jingyan" (Land investigation experiences in the vicinity of Bosheng city). Hongse Zhonghua (Red China) 115 and 116 (Oct. 3 and 6). CC Reel 17.

*Western-Language Titles*

BRANDT, Conrad, Benjamin SCHWARTZ and John FAIRBANK (1966) A Documentary History of Chinese Communism. New York: Atheneum.

CHAO KUO-CHUN (1960) Agrarian Policy of the Chinese Communist Party, 1921-1959. New Delhi: Asia Publishing House.

CHESNEAUX, Jean (ed.) (1972) Popular Movements and Secret Societies in China, 1840-1950. Stanford: Stanford University Press.

(1971) Secret Societies in China in the 19th and 20th Centuries. Hong Kong: Heinemann Educational Books.

CRESSEY, G.B. (1955) Land of the 500 Million: A Geography of China. New York: McGraw Hill.

DAVIN, Delia (1976) Woman-Work: Women and the Party in Revolutionary China. London: Oxford University Press.

DELIUSIN, L.P. (1975) "The sixth congress of the Chinese Communist Party and its agrarian-peasant program." Chinese Studies in History 8, 3 (spring): 45-114. Translated from Chapter 8 of Agrano-krest'ianskii vopros v politike KPK (1921-1928) [The Agrarian-Peasant Question in the Policies of the CCP, (1921-1928)]. Moscow: "Nauka" Publishing House, 1972. 376-439.

DONOVAN, Peter W. (1976) The Red Army in Kiangsi, 1931-1934. Ithaca: Cornell China-Japan Progam.

DORRILL, W.F. (1974) "Rewriting history to further Maoism: the Ningtu conference of 1932" in J.C. Hsiung, ed. The Logic of 'Maoism': Critiques and Explication. New York: Praeger, 62-85.

GRIGOR'EV, A.M. (1975) "An important landmark in the history of the Chinese Communist Party." Chinese Studies in History 8, 3 (spring): 18-44. Translated from "Vazhnaia vekha v istorii KPK," Problemy dal'nego vostoka [Problems of the Far East], 1973, no. 2.

GROVE, L. (1975) "Creating a northern soviet." Modern China 1, 3 (July): 243-270.

HAN SUYIN (1972) The Morning Deluge: Mao Tsetung and the

Chinese Revolution, 1893-1954. Boston: Little Brown.

HARRISON, John (1972) The Long March to Power: A History of the Chinese Communist Party, 1921-1972. New York: Praeger.

HSIAO TSO-LIANG (1969) The Land Revolution in China, 1930-1934. A Study of Documents. Seattle: University of Washington Press.

(1961) Power Relations within the Chinese Communist Movement, 1930-1934. Seattle: University of Washington Press.

HSIEH, W. (1972) "Triads, salt smugglers, and local uprisings: observations on the social and economic background of the Waichow revolution of 1911" in Chesneaux (1972): 145-164.

HU CHI-HSI (1975) "The sexual revolution in the Kiangsi soviet." China Q. 59 (July-Sept.): 477-490.

HUANG, P.C. (1975) "Mao Tse-tung and the middle peasants." Modern China 1, 3: 271-296.

ISAACS, Harold R. (1961) The Tradegy of the Chinese Revolution. Stanford: Stanford University Press.

KIM, Ilpyong J. (1973) The Politics of Chinese Communism: Kiangsi Under the Soviets. Berkeley: University of California Press.

KLEIN, Donald W. and Anne C. CLARK (1971) Biographic Dictionary of Chinese Communism. Cambridge, Mass.: Harvard University Press.

KUO, W. (1966) "Chinese communist 6th central committee's 4th plenum and party rift." Issues and Studies 3, 1 (October).

LEE SHU-CHING (1951) "Employment conditions of the agricultural laborer in China and his prospects for social advancement." Rural Sociology 16, 3 (Sept.): 238-245.

LÖTVEIT, Trygve (1973) Chinese Communism, 1931-1934: Experience in Civil Government. Lund, Sweden: Studentlitteratur.

LUST, J. (1972) "Secret societies, popular movements, and the 1911 revolution," in Chesneaux (1972): 165-200.

MAO ZE-DONG (1967) Selected Works of Mao Tse-tung. Beijing: Foreign Languages Press. 4 vols.

(1965) Selected Works of Mao Tse-tung. Beijing: Foreign Languages Press. 4 vols.

(1956.4.25) "On the ten major relationships." Peking Review 1, (1977): 10-25.

(1945) "Resolutions on some questions in the history of our party" in Selected Works of Mao Tse-tung. Vol. 4. London: Lawrence and Wishart, 1954-56: 171-218.

(1934.1.27) "Be concerned with the well-being of the masses, pay attention to methods of work" in Mao (1967), Vol. I: 147-152. Also in Mao (1972), Vol. IV: 219-282.

(1934.1.23) "Our economic policy" in Mao (1967), Vol. I: 141-145.

(1933.8.20) "Pay attention to economic work" in Mao (1967) Vol. I: 129-136.

MARX, Karl (1967) Capital: A Critique of Political Economy. Vol. 1. New York: International Publishers.

MARX, K. and F. ENGELS (1968) "Manifesto of the communist party" in Karl Marx and Frederick Engels, Selected Works. New York: International Publishers.

ROY, M.N. (1946) Revolution and Counter-Revolution in China. Calcutta: Renaissance Publishers.

RUE, John E. (1966) Mao Tse-tung in Opposition, 1927-1935. Stanford: Stanford University Press.

SCHRAM, S. (1966) "Mao Tse-tung and secret societies." China Q. 27 (July-Sept.): 1-13.

SHENG YUEH (1971) Sun Yat-sen University in Moscow and the Chinese Revolution. A Personal Account. New York: Paragon Book Gallery, Ltd.

SMEDLEY, Agnes (1956) The Great Road: The Life and Times of Chu Teh. New York: Monthly Review Press.

(1936) China's Red Army Marches. London: Lawrence and Wishart, Ltd.

SNOW, Edgar (1938) Red Star Over China. New York: Random House.

STARR, J. (1976) "From the 10th party congress to the premiership of Hua Kuo-feng: the significance of the colour of the cat." China Q. 67 (Sept.): 457-488.

SULESKI, R.S. (1968) "The Fu-ti'an Incident, December 1930" in R. Suleski and D.H. Bays, Early Communist China: Two Studies. Ann Arbor: Center for Chinese Studies.

SUN SHAO-TSENG (1938) "Landownership and its concentration in China" in Institute of Pacific Relations (ed.) Agrarian China: 1-5. Chicago: University of Chicago Press.

SWARUP, Shanti (1966) A Study of the Chinese Communist Movement. London: Oxford University Press.

WALLER, Derek J. (1972) The Kiangsi Soviet Republic: Mao and the National Congresses of 1931 and 1934. Berkeley: Center for Chinese Studies.

WU TIEN-WEI (1972 [?]) A Selected and Annotated Bibliography of the Ch'en Ch'eng Collection. Unpublished.

——— (1970) "The Kiangsi soviet period, a bibliographic review on the Ch'en Ch'eng collection." Journal of Asian Studies 29, 2 (Feb.): 395-412.

YAKHONTOFF, Victor A. (1934) The Chinese Soviets. New York: Coward-McCann.

# Glossary

Agricultural Laborer Unions (Gunong gonghui) 雇农工会

Bo Gu (Qin Bang-xian) 博古（秦邦宪）

Caixi township 才溪乡

(CCP) Central Bureau of the Soviet Areas (Zhonggong suqu zhongyangju) 中共苏区中央局

Central Executive Committee (Zhongyang zhixing weiyuanhui) 中央执行委员会

Central Soviet Area (Zhongyang suqu) 中央苏区

Changgang township 长冈乡

Chang Han 长汉

Changjiao village 长窖村

Chen Cheng 陈诚

Chen Gun-tong 陈赓同

Chen Qi-han 陈奇涵

Chen Xiang-zhi (Chen Zan-xian) 陈象质（陈赞贤）

Chen Yi 陈毅

Children's Corps (Ertong tuan) 儿童团

chipin 赤贫

| | |
|---|---|
| *chouduo bushao* | 抽多补少 |
| *choufei bushou* | 抽肥补瘦 |
| Committee for the Improvement of Women's Living Conditions (Funü shenghuo gaishan weiyuanhui) | 妇女生活改善委员会 |
| Congress of Red Army Family Members (Hongjun juanshu daibiao dahui) | 红军眷属代表大会 |
| Congress of Women Workers and Peasant Women (Nügong nongfu daibiaohui) | 女工农妇代表会 |
| Council of People's Commissars (Renmin weiyuanhui) | 人民委员会 |
| county (xian) | 县 |
| district (qu) | 区 |
| Donggu county | 东固县 |
| Duan Qi-feng | 段起凤 |
| First National Congress of Soviet Deputies (Diyici quanguo suweiai daibiao dahui) | 第一次全国苏维埃代表大会 |
| Futian | 宋田 |
| Gan River | 赣江 |
| Ganzhou | 赣州 |
| Gelao Hui | 哥老会 |
| *gong(ren)-gu(nong)-ku(li)* | 工(人).雇(农).苦(力) |

| | |
|---|---|
| Gonglue county | 公略县 |
| Guangchang county | 广昌县 |
| He Long | 贺龙 |
| Hengshan county | 衡山县 |
| Huang Gong-lue | 黄公略 |
| Jinggangshan | 井冈山 |
| Jingweituan | 靖卫团 |
| Kang Ke-qing | 康克清 |
| Land Investigation Movement (Chatian yundong) | 查田运动 |
| Li Li-san | 李立三 |
| Liu Di | 刘敌 |
| Liu Shao-biao | 刘绍彪 |
| Liu Shao-ming | 刘绍明 |
| Liu Zhi-dan | 刘志丹 |
| Lü Xian | 吕咸 |
| Meixian | 梅县 |
| Meng Qing-shu | 孟庆树 |
| Movement to Construct the Soviets (Suweiai jianshe yundong) | 苏维埃建设运动 |
| Ningdu (Bosheng) county | 宁都（博生）县 |

| | |
|---|---|
| Peng De-huai | 彭德怀 |
| Peng Zi-zhong | 彭子忠 |
| Poor Peasant Association (Pinnong hui) | 贫农会 |
| Poor Peasant Corps (Pinnong tuan) | 贫农团 |
| Provincial Congress of Women Workers and Peasant Women (Quansheng nügong nongfu daibiao huiyi) | 全省女工农妇代表会议 |
| Qing Bang | 青邦 |
| Qu Qiu-bai | 瞿秋白 |
| Red Guard Squad (Chiwei dui) | 赤卫队 |
| Ruan Xiao-xian | 阮啸仙 |
| Ruijin | 瑞金 |
| Sandian Hui | 三点会 |
| Shaan-Gan-Ning | 陕甘宁 |
| Shangshe district | 上社区 |
| Shi-sou ziliao shi | 石叟资料室 |
| Soviet (suweiai) | 苏维埃 |
| Taihe county | 泰和县 |
| Township (*xiang*) | 乡 |

| | |
|---|---|
| village *(cun)* | 村 |
| Wang Ming (Chen Shao-yu) | 王明(陈绍禹) |
| Wang Zhen-ren | 王振仁 |
| Wang Zuo | 王佐 |
| Xiao Zhi-chun | 肖志春 |
| Xie Ying-shan | 谢应山 |
| *yicang* | 义仓 |
| Yongfeng district | 永丰区 |
| *youmin* | 沇民 |
| *youmin wuchanjieji* | 沇民无产阶级 |
| Young Pioneers (Shaonian xianfeng dui) | 少年先锋队 |
| Yuan Wen-cai | 袁文才 |
| Zeng Li-bang | 曾礼邦 |
| Zhang Qing-qiu | 张琴秋 |
| Zhang Wen-tian (Luo Fu) | 张闻天(洛甫) |
| Zhu Da-xi | 朱大喜 |
| Zou Li-dong | 邹丽东 |